HOPE SPRINGS ETERNAL

HOPE SPRINGS ETERNAL

With contributions from:

Cardinal Vincent Nichols (Foreword), Bishop Erik Varden & Nordic Bishops' Conference, Fr Patrick van der Vorst, Joanna Bogle, Mgr John Devine, Fr Simon Francis Gaine, O.P, Canon Philip Gillespie, Sir Stephen Hough, Bishop Graham James, Alderman Vincent Keaveny, Fr Toby Lees, O.P, Bishop Jane Mainwaring, Revd Dr Rob Marshall, Fr Stephen Morrison, O. Praem, Canon John O'Leary, Darren Perks, Fr Dominic Robinson S.J., Bishop John Sherrington, Fr Robert Smialek, Sandy Walkington, Francesca Weal, Fr Nigel Woolen, Richard Jacques and Archbishop Joseph Marino.

Compiled by Daniel P. Cronin

First published in Great Britain in 2025 by ST PAULS Publishing.

187 Battersea Bridge Road, London, SW11 3AS, United Kingdom, Ph: +44 (0)207978 4300, www.stpauls.org.uk.

ST PAULS Publishing, Moyglare Road, Maynooth, Co. Kildare, Ireland, Ph: + 353 (1) 628 5933, www.stpauls.ie.

A CIP catalogue record for this book is available from the British Library.

ISBN: 978-1-910365-93-9

Typeset and Cover Design by ST PAULS Publishing.

Printed and bound in the UK by Bishops Printers

ST PAULS is an activity of the priests and brothers of the Society of St Paul who proclaim the Gospel through the media of social communication.

Contents

Introduction and Acknowledgements

In the seminary, we were encouraged to read widely. One of the books that made a great impression on me was written by Viktor Frankl entitled: *Man's Search for Meaning*. Frankl was an Austrian psychologist and philosopher but more pertinently he was a Holocaust survivor. He observed in the concentration camps that those who survived were people who retained hope.

What comes to the fore in this collection of essays is that in some ways hope could be considered the Cinderella of the virtues. 'In short, there are three things that last: faith, hope and love; and the greatest of these is love' (1 Cor 13:13). Yet hope is vital for us as we journey through life. It is more than opportune that our Holy Father Pope Francis has chosen to draw our focus to the need for us to be pilgrims of hope during the Jubilee Year 2025 and beyond and urge our prayers for the same.

We need prophets of hope for our times. One such prophet is Cardinal Pierbattista Pizzaballa, the Latin Patriarch of Jerusalem, Grand Prior of the Knights and Dames of the Holy Sepulchre. His courageous leadership is phenomenal. A man convinced of the power of prayer he both leads his people and is equally inspired by them, particularly by those living in Gaza at this most challenging of times. He is inspired by their hope for the future and their lack of a sense of vengeance, rooted and anchored as they are in the Lord Jesus.

I wish to express my profound gratitude to each of the contributors to this volume, all of whom are busy people but were prepared to write for this collection within a very short time frame. I am honoured that Cardinal Vincent Nichols has provided the Foreword and for his affirmation of this Project. I am especially grateful to Archbishop Joseph Marino for his permission to include the text of a lecture he gave in Birmingham, Alabama where he is now retired following a very distinguished Vatican diplomatic ministry culminating in his appointment as President of the Ecclesiastical Academy in Rome where our future Papal Nuncios are trained. In the same measure, I express my appreciation to Bishop Erik Varden OCSO, President of the Nordic Bishops Conference who, along with his episcopal confreres, has graciously given his approval for the inclusion of their Pastoral Letter for the Jubilee Year in this anthology.

I trust and pray that you will find intellectual stimulation from reading the articles that follow and be spiritually nourished by what our authors have shared so generously. May this Jubilee Year be a time of grace, hope and joy for you.

Canon Daniel Cronin
Knebworth, Hertfordshire

Foreword

In proclaiming 2025 as a Jubilee Year Pope Francis opened his announcement with the words 'Hope does not disappoint' (*Spes Non Confundit,* quoting Romans 5:5). The Holy Father continued: 'For everyone, may the Jubilee be a moment of a genuine, personal encounter with the Lord Jesus, the "door" (cf. John 10:7.9) of our salvation, whom the Church is charged to proclaim always, everywhere and to all as "our hope" (1 Timothy 1:1)'.

I welcome this volume with its title *Hope Springs Eternal,* confident that it will stimulate our appreciation of the great virtue of hope.

Pope Francis went on to write:

'Hope is born of love and based on the love springing from the pierced heart of Jesus upon the cross: "For if while we were enemies, we were reconciled to God through the death of his Son, much more surely, having been reconciled, will we be saved by his life" (Romans 5:19). That life becomes manifest in our own life of faith, which begins with Baptism, develops in openness to God's grace and is enlivened by a hope constantly renewed and confirmed by the working of the Holy Spirit.'

The various contributions to this anthology will enrich our pilgrimage not only during this Holy Year but also throughout our lives. The most radical hope we are given is, of course, the hope of heaven. We live through all the uncertainties of this life with the firm and sure grasp of the hope of heaven as the final destiny of our earthly pilgrimage.

I thank all who have contributed to the book for all they have given us. I pray that it will bear fruit in our lives and throughout this most blessed year.

+ Vincent Nichols

Bishop Erik Varden and
the Nordic Bishops' Conference

Iubilaeum MMXXV

Our Holy Father Pope Francis has proclaimed the year 2025 a Jubilee Year. It is a wonderful gift to the Church, indeed to the whole world. The Jubilee is a Biblical institution. We read of it first in Leviticus — not perhaps the book we most readily turn to for spiritual reading. So let us remind ourselves of what the Lord told Moses on Mount Sinai regarding the year of a Jubilee.

The Jubilee was to take place every fiftieth year, after 'seven weeks of years'. Its function was to give all people resident in the Land a regular, predictable chance to redress balances, release captives, cancel debts, and enjoy corporate rest. It was to be a year of homecoming. 'In this year of Jubilee you shall return, every one of you, to your property' (Lev 25.12). This point regards more than just a sentimental attachment to the old camp fire. It regards the nature of property and our claim to it. Leviticus recognizes the complex dynamics of human communities. It may happen through various transactions that territories pass from hand to hand. Someone lives on the land for a while, then sells it, or is driven off; somebody else redeems or occupies it. Conflicts do arise. Someone cries from the left: 'This land is mine!' Somebody else cries from the right, 'No way! It is mine!' This is the sort of situation the Biblical text addresses. It does so by short-circuiting the discourse of rights and entitlement. 'The land', says the Lord, ‘shall not be sold in perpetuity, for the land is mine; with me you are but aliens and tenants’ (Lev 25.23).

Given the parlous state of our world right now, this perspective is important. A durable society, teeming with women and men who are truly free, corresponding to God’s will for humanity, cannot be built simply on claims to possession. For a society to thrive, its individuals must first become a *people,* bound together by a covenant of justice consonant with natural and divinely inspired law. Ultimately, we are all, like Abraham, our father in faith, strangers and aliens in the land (cf Gen 23:4). We must learn, then, to be worthy sojourners, committed at once to righteousness and to hospitality, mindful that the land, wherever on the globe we may happen to live, remains the Lord’s, and that we shall be called to account for our political, religious, and ecological stewardship of it.

Having established the principle concerning ownership of land, Leviticus applies the Jubilee concept more intimately to human relationships. The Bible has no illusions about this, singing as it does of ‘how good and pleasant it is when brothers live in unity’ (Ps 133:1) recognizing even as it acknowledges that such unity does not come cheap. It must be striven for, sometimes at the cost of great suffering. Let us not forget that the history of our race outside Eden begins with fratricide (Gen 4:1-8). It is not natural for us human beings, as long as our nature is wounded and blinded by sin, to live peaceably together. That is why peace, in Scripture, is presented as dynamic, a living reality we must *pursue* by departing from evil and by doing good (cf Ps 34:14). On account of life’s vicissitudes it may occur that one human being becomes subject to another — say, on account of debt or imprisonment. The one who holds in his hand the bill of debt or the gaoler’s key may feel, then, an intoxicating rush of power, as if the other's dependents belonged to him and were his to deal with as he pleases. Leviticus reminds us that this is a perverse illusion. Even 'if your brother becomes poor beside you, and sells himself to you', we are told, 'you shall not make him serve as a slave' (Lev 25:39). No human being can, on any terms, pretend to own another. Men and women sometimes do stupid, even wicked things. They may need to be compelled by just means to pay back what they owe; they may need to be chastized or restrained. But they remain sovereign. What is more, they are by virtue of their simple humanity, made in God's image, bearers of an immense potential dignity we owe it to them to recognize, acknowledge and to call forth. Leviticus undermines the idea that some people are naturally others' subjects by decreeing that all bondsmen are to be set free in the year of a Jubilee. 'For they are my servants', says the Lord, 'whom I brought out of the land of Egypt' and redeemed (Lev 25:42). Only God can rightly say to us, 'You are mine' (cf Isa 43:1). Only he, who is almighty *and* merciful, can let us experience total dependence as perfect freedom.

The ideal put before us by the Bible is not upheld in the world we inhabit. This is a state of affairs we must, as Christians, confront and strive by every means to change. Just think: human trafficking, a terrible and demeaning trade, is virtually soaring; whole nations are crippled by debt and ruthlessly exploited; commercial agencies (above and below board) promote and foster addiction to drugs, games, pornography and booze for the sole purpose of gain, *devising* ways of keeping people shackled. And what are we to say of the erosion of the rights of the unborn, increasingly denied any form of humane, legal protection under law? When our countries were evangelized a millennium or so ago, a major civilizational step forward was the recognition of each person's sovereign dignity, which was seen to begin in the womb. Belief in an incarnate God, made a man like us in all things but sin' (Eucharistic Prayer IV), had a profound impact on our collective understanding of what it is to be human. The further this belief recedes from public life, the more is humanity under threat. An individual can then once again consider another individual his or her chattel. This is a tendency we are morally obliged to counter constructively as we uphold an anthropology worthy of our nature.

It is providentially wonderful that next year's Jubilee, summoning us to construct a more just world, coincides with the seventeenth centenary of the Council of Nicaea, held in 325. At Nicaea the creed was defined that we still profess each Sunday, when we affirm our belief in the Blessed Trinity, one God in three Persons and three persons in one God; in the incarnation of God's Son, 'Light from Light, true God from true God'; in Jesus Christ's redeeming and sanctifying work through his birth, teaching, death, resurrection, and ascension into heaven; and in the transforming presence among and within us of the Holy Spirit, the Comforter, who spoke through the prophets and speaks to us still through Holy Mother, Church.

As your bishops, we pray that the Jubilee year may see an effective, cordial, and intelligent deepening of faith in our countries. We invite you to return to the sources of our creed by studying the Scriptures and our wonderful Catholic Catechism in order thereby to be rooted more deeply in the mystery of faith, to experience what it means to live 'in Christ' (cf Gal 2.20), better placed to 'give an account of the hope that is in you' (1 Pet 3:15). Thus prepared we shall find the strength and means to be agents of the Jubilee, so that the Lord may, through us, as we pray each Good

Friday, 'cleanse the world of all errors, banish disease, drive out hunger, unlock prisons, loosen fetters, granting to travellers safety, to pilgrims return, health to the sick, and salvation to the dying'. We will support you in this holy endeavour with all our strength, grateful for the witness of fidelity, charity, and generosity we find in the dioceses it is our privilege to serve. In his letter announcing the Jubilee, published on the feast of Our Lady of Lourdes 2022, the Holy Father expressed hope that this forthcoming year may build up the Church 'so that it can press forward in its mission of bringing the joyful proclamation of the Gospel to all'. To this intention we say wholeheartedly: 'Amen!' The Jubilee motto is '*Peregrinantes in spem*' [Pilgrims in hope]. We are, that is, to be pilgrims moving out of hopelessness into hope. As we embark on another Advent, we marvel at the grace given us in the Word's incarnation, which renews the world. May we credibly witness to this newness as Christ's disciples through generous charity, firm communion and brave justice, illumined by the splendour of Truth.

Bishop Erik Varden and the Nordic Bishops' Conference

Friend of the Humble (Supper at Emmaus)
Painted by Léon-Augustin L'Hermitte (1824-1925),
Painted in 1892,
Oil on canvas
© Museum of Fine Arts, Boston

Fr Patrick van der Vorst

Christian Hope Shines as a Beacon

Hope is one of the foundational virtues of the Christian life, sitting alongside faith and love as gifts that sustain and guide us. It is the quiet yet powerful assurance that God's promises are trustworthy, His love is unfailing, and His plans are ultimately good. In a world that so often feels burdened by uncertainty and fear, Christian hope shines as a beacon, lifting our hearts and drawing our eyes towards God's providence.

If I had to choose one Gospel passage that encapsulates Christian hope most beautifully, it would undoubtedly be the story of the Road to Emmaus, found in Luke 24:13-35. This remarkable narrative, which unfolds straight after the Resurrection, captures the essence of what Christian hope is about—not as a fleeting sentiment, but as a transformative encounter with the risen Christ that changes everything. The story begins with two disciples walking away from Jerusalem, their hearts heavy with disappointment and grief, as the one they had hoped would redeem Israel has been crucified. All their dreams and expectations lie shattered, and even the mysterious news of an empty tomb has failed to reignite their faith. Their walk to Emmaus is not just a physical journey; it is a spiritual retreat into hopelessness. They are, in many ways, representative of anyone who has experienced loss or disillusionment, unable to see beyond the immediate pain to the greater work of God.

In the midst of their despair, a stranger joins them on the road. The reader knows this is Jesus, but the disciples do not recognize Him. He listens as they pour out their sorrow, meeting them in their brokenness without immediately revealing who He is. Then, in a moment that marks the turning point of the story, Jesus begins to open the Scriptures to them, showing how everything that had happened—the suffering and death they found so incomprehensible—was in fact part of the larger plan of God. He places their story within the context of salvation history, and in doing so, their hearts begin to burn within them. That is hope for me: this burning fire, this burning love for God! This is the first great lesson of the Emmaus story: hope is rekindled when we allow God to place our experiences, especially our suffering, into the context of His greater plan. Christian hope does not deny the reality of pain or pretend that everything is fine. Rather, it is the trust that God is present in our struggles and is weaving them into His redemptive story. We become an active part of his story. Full participants.

As soon as the disciples recognize Jesus, He vanishes from their sight. This does not leave them despondent; rather, they are energized and transformed. They immediately return to Jerusalem, filled with joy and ready to share the good news: "The Lord has risen!" Jesus wasn't physically present anymore, yet he was more present that ever in their hearts. Here we see another key dimension of hope at work. It is not a passive virtue that leaves us stagnant. True Christian hope propels us outward, it pushes us forward.

Léon-Augustin L'Hermitte's 1892 painting, *A Friend of the Humble* (Supper at Emmaus), housed in the Museum of

Fine Arts in Boston, is a remarkable interpretation of our Gospel story. It depicts the moment when the risen Christ is recognised by His disciples in the breaking of bread. What sets this work apart is how L'hermitte blends the biblical narrative with a contemporary 19th century setting, making the scene both timeless and deeply relevant to contemporary viewers when it was painted.

The painting shows three generations of a family—child, parents, and grandparents—sharing a simple meal with Christ seated among them. The warmth and intimacy of the scene radiate from the canvas. Unlike traditional portrayals of Jesus as majestic and distant, L'hermitte presents Him as approachable and human, emphasizing the core Christian truth that Jesus walked among us, sharing in the ordinary moments of life with ordinary people. The title, *Friend of the Humble,* captures this beautifully.

The painting drew high praise from Vincent van Gogh, one of L'Hermitte's admirers. Van Gogh wrote: *"For years I have not seen anything as beautiful as this scene by L'Hermitte."* This endorsement highlights the emotional and theological depth of the work, which blends realism with a spiritual message that transcends its time. It is profoundly compelling that Vincent van Gogh, a deeply spiritual and introspective artist, felt such a profound connection with this painting. Here we see one great creative soul resonating with another's masterpiece, bridging their unique yet kindred expressions of faith and humanity. This is more than admiration—it's a meeting of artistic and spiritual worlds, where van Gogh recognized in L'Hermitte's work the same search for the divine in the ordinary that shaped his own art.

The Road to Emmaus is not just a story about something that happened long ago. It is a blueprint for the Christian life, a reminder that we are all on a journey where Christ walks beside us. It invites us to open our hearts to the Word of God, to recognize Christ in the breaking of bread, and to trust that He is leading us to the fulfilment of His promises. Christian hope assures us that even when the road seems long and the destination unclear, we are not alone. We have to remember though that hope is not something we generate on our own. It is a gift. A gift rooted in the victory of Christ and sustained by His presence. Whatever burdens we carry or uncertainties we face, the Emmaus story reminds us that we are part of a larger narrative, one that ends not in despair but in resurrection. Hope lifts our eyes to this horizon and keeps us moving forward, trusting that the best is yet to come. Christian hope therefore is not wishful thinking or blind optimism. It is the unshakable confidence that the risen Christ walks with us, even in our darkest moments. It propels us forward, ignites our hearts, and transforms despair into purpose.

Fr Patrick van der Vorst, Precentor of Westminster Cathedral. Author and founder of the Christian Art app

Joanna Bogle

HOPE as a Call to Courage

When I was a Girl Guide, we learned that "A Guide smiles and sings under all difficulties". It's probably been changed now with some sort of therapy-talk added – but it did offer a practical way of approaching challenges presented by camping and cooking over open fires in pouring rain and so on.

One result of the upbeat approach is that I am, as an adult, a rather annoying woman when faced with gloom and despondency in general, and with speculation about the future more specifically. Combined with a lifetime's interest in history, it has given me an irritating tendency to see things in the longer term - especially things connected with the Church.

The virtue of hope is not connected with optimism – and nor, for what it's worth, was that Girl Guide rule. Hope, as the useful summary given in the *Compendium of the Catechism of the Catholic Church* puts it, "is the theological virtue by which we desire and await from God eternal life as our happiness, placing our trust in Christ's promises and relying on the help of the grace of the Holy Spirit to merit it and to persevere to the end of our earthly life" (388).

Such hope enables us, and the Church, to see things in their proper perspective – and to deal with what is necessary at any given time. When Saint Augustine of Hippo (d 430

AD) looked at the collapsing Roman Empire, he did not gloat with gloom but instead wrote a masterpiece, *The City of God*, which so many centuries later still speak to us. He could not have known that another Augustine, some 150 years later, would land on the shores of remote Kent in response to the plea of a Gaulish girl married to a pagan Saxon king, and begin the conversion of England.

Augustine of Canterbury (d c 604) could not have known that a later English king, inheritor of centuries of Catholic tradition and a self-proclaimed full supporter of the Church, would destroy England's monasteries, sever the link with Rome, and establish complications that would reverberate through years and years of bitterness and division. Nor could anyone during all those years, including heroic martyrs who died for the Faith, know that all sorts of extraordinary events would, in the 21st century, move onwards to new goodwill and the attendance of a future king at the canonization in Rome of an English saint (Cardinal Saint John Henry Newman, d 1890, canonized 2018) …

And so, it goes on. In the early 1970s there was a general feeling that Communism, although a grim creed focused on an atheistic view and offering nothing practical in the way of human benefits, was probably here to stay and that the people of, for example, Poland, had better accept the fact. No one expected the election of a Polish Pope. In that extraordinary year of three Popes in 1978, I remember, in the offices of a Catholic newspaper, sorting all the cuttings we had about the various Cardinals who might possibly be *papabile.* They were mostly Italian, of course – though as a matter of courtesy we added our own Cardinal Hume, and then, rummaging through the files, any others with names that were familiar to us. There was Warsaw's heroic Cardinal Wyszynski of course, who had been imprisoned in the Stalin years and was now elderly – but who was this other "W", with an unpronounceable name, the Archbishop of Krakow?

When Pope John Paul II addressed the world, he urged us all "Do not be afraid!"- a message that entirely resonates with the Church's teaching on hope. And, in our imperfect and muddled world, it's a message that we need again and again. When he came to Britain, and had tea with the Queen, there was something almost absurd in how simple it looked (it wasn't, of course: there had been great negotiations, not least because of the Falklands war…) and it left a glow that enabled a further papal visit – a State Visit at Her Majesty's warm invitation – and so history goes on.

Christian hope is emphatically not, however, about things-coming-all-right-in-the-end in history, because they simply don't. A friend discovered a useful quotation which sums things up, when we were discussing all this. "It'll all come right in the end…and it hasn't come right, so it's evidently not the end!" There are times when good things happen, when we should rightly rejoice, when justice triumphs or when we get a glimpse of God's huge generosity and care for us. There are times when what might seem thrilling and exciting somehow goes all wrong. There are times when our own understanding is limited and our emotions are not the best judge of what is best for us.

The hope we have in God, the hope which the Church commends as a central and important virtue, is about trusting in God and looking to eternity. It's not a cheery tool to which we can resort when things feel bleak: it is rather the way we should see things as part of Christ's own body, his Church. His suffering on the Cross and his Resurrection are central to the promises he has given to us and of which, in the ancient and traditional prayer, we ask to be worthy.

Smiling and singing through difficulties doesn't always work – some things, like toothache or heartache, need practical help and attention. We must help one another – and that's part of the hope and mercy that the Church teaches us as well. But the call to Christian hope is, in an important sense, also a call to courage, to see things through to the end, not to give way to despair. I am glad I was given, in addition to hearty Girl Guide fare, instruction from the Church in the virtue of Hope.

Joanna Bogle is an Historian, lecturer and author of some 20 books.

Monsignor John Devine

Hope in a Troubled World

I was shocked at the dinner table recently to hear the extreme views of another guest. What really shocked me wasn't even the views expressed but the assumption that I shared them. No longer can I expect agreement among 'normal' people on the basic issues facing us today. The convention never to discuss politics or religion has never been more necessary.

Covid and Brexit are obvious areas of disagreement, but the battle lines spread wider. The post war consensus has given way to polarization and populism in the countries to which we once looked as the exemplars of democracy. We saw ourselves as models to which the rest of the world could aspire. One jewel in the crown was the National Health Service – the great equalizer. Some now celebrate its shortcomings as an opportunity to revert to a system where those who can afford it get the best care. Calls to restrict university education to a privileged minority gain ground even though in many European countries it remains free.

We live in a troubled world. Appalling loss of life in the Middle East and Ukraine is matched by industrial scale atrocities in Sudan. Lives lost through bombs and missiles are matched by the calamities of climate change. Mass migration is an inevitable consequence of both evils. Social media has become the vehicle for those who would like to turn back the clock, propagate extreme views and blame the losers.

Christ's mission was frustrated, opposed and crushed. The words of the disciples on the road to Emmaus say it all: 'Our own hope had been that he would be the one to set Israel free' (*Lk 24:13-35*); hopes dashed with the execution of their leader and friend. Scurrying away from Jerusalem they probably thought 'They'll come after us next'. The enemies of Jesus had prevailed. He was a loser and they were losers, too.

We rejoice when our point of view prevails. We sink into depression when 'the other side' seems to be winning. Even sport has become tribal. How do we bridge the gaps between winners and losers? What's the grown-up way of not merely surviving but flourishing in the 21st century? The Gospels give us lessons in how to do this.

Mark relates how James and John request a seat at his right and left hand when Jesus succeeds to his kingdom (*Mk 10:40*). In Matthew, it's their mother who speaks on their behalf (*Mt 20:20*). Their fellow disciples are indignant. Jesus tells them, 'Among the pagans their so-called rulers make their authority felt.... This is not to happen among you' (*Mk10:43*). James and John (and their mother) operate according to the "winners and losers" model. Jesus challenges this.

How often does Jesus begin his teaching with the words 'The Kingdom of heaven is like...'? He doesn't tell us how to live but invites us to recognize alternative ways of looking at life. His parables allow us to see life through God's eyes. Jesus doesn't judge or condemn. He demonstrates how the pagan way doesn't work. Every parable contains a surprise. Each story contradicts the way the 'pagans' operate. It's also the way the Scribes and Pharisees think: reward or punishment. And that's the way I think and operate most of the time. I profess the gospel with my lips while attempting to promote the Kingdom according to the world's way of doing things. I'll even use violence (as a last resort, of course) and assume that God is on my side, the winning side. Jesus doesn't want us to side with the winners. He himself doesn't. He sides with the losers. They flocked to him.

The parable of the wheat and the darnel suggests we don't need to choose sides, to intervene, otherwise both good and bad will be destroyed together: 'Let them both grow till the harvest' (*Mt 13:24-33*). Letting go requires faith. Jesus says, 'If your brother wrongs you seven times a day and seven times comes back to you and says "I am sorry", you must forgive him.' For the disciples that's a tall order. Their immediate response is to ask: 'Increase our faith'. Jesus tells them they have faith enough already: 'Were your faith the size of a mustard seed you could say to this mulberry tree, "Be uprooted and planted in the sea". And it would obey you' (*Lk 17:4-6*). A little bit of faith is all it takes.

Faith and hope are related. Both are gifts of the Spirit. Christian hope is more than 'looking on the bright side'. It's not about feelings or mood or cheering ourselves up. Maintaining hope in the face of difficulty, negativity and violence requires faith in the promises of Christ. For the Christian it's based on the central narrative of our faith: Christ died and rose again. We look forward to our own resurrection, too. But there'll be lots of little deaths and resurrections before then. Our celebration of the Eucharist reminds us of this every step of the way. Just like the disciples on the Road to Emmaus, we recognize him in the breaking of bread.

Monsignor John Devine OBE, Parish Priest and Dean, Cathedral Church of Saint Mary of the Isle, Douglas, Isle of Man

Fr Simon Francis Gaine, O.P.

We Hope Because He hoped

Jesus Christ is our hope. We hope in Christ and we hope because of him. He is the Saviour who has freed us from whatever frustrates our hope, and he draws our hearts and minds to where all true hope points. He leads us in hope towards full happiness in God, together with the joy of the whole company of saints.

Yet we also hope because Christ himself hoped. While he lived and breathed and walked among us on earth, there was hope in Christ's heart, and his hope reaches across time to us who hope in his love today. His death destroys our death, his rising restores us to life, and his hope brings hope to our hearts. His hope inspires us today, and sustains us each and every day. His hope takes us by the hand to bring us to the light of eternal day. There is no act of true hope that we make, as we journey to his Father and our Father, that does not find its source and nourishment in him.

The Word did not take flesh without assuming our human difficulties and challenges. He certainly did not assume our rebellion and sin, but he shared our mortality and vulnerability. He always remained one with his Father, but he became one with us in our suffering and in death. But in the midst of all this he hoped for what he did not already possess, hoped for the joy of resurrection and for us to be united with him. He shared our difficulties and our tragedies so that we might share his hope and so enter into his glory.

In the Garden of Gethsemane, Jesus sought of his Father that the cup he was to drink might pass him by. His body but naturally revolted at his impending suffering and death; hence his plea. And this desire was perfectly rational. We do not want suffering as such and we do not want death in itself, and neither did Christ so want them. To desire suffering and death in themselves is senseless. It was his rational will that the cup of suffering and death pass him by.

Yet in the difficulties he faced, as he prayed in the Garden, already abandoned by his disciples but not by his Father, he was sustained by hope. He had already prophesied his betrayal, suffering and death. He had already foretold his resurrection on the third day. Now, sustained by hope in the joy that was set before him, he chose that the Father's will, not his own will, should be done. He hoped not for death, but for resurrection; he hoped not for suffering, but that we would benefit from his Cross. Out of hope, he gave himself for us all.

It was not simply that Christ wanted to go to the Father. It was not just that he liked the idea of ascending to heaven. It was that he hoped with all his heart, while he lived this mortal life with us. Hoping is more than wanting, just as wanting is more than liking. There are things I like, things that I like to eat and pleasures I enjoy. But just because I like them doesn't mean I want them right at this moment. Wanting or desiring is more than liking.

But hoping is also more than wanting. To act in hope is to do more than act out of desire. Hope kicks in when things become difficult, when life gets challenging, when what we want is not easily obtained. That's when hope can sustain us in the midst of the obstacle course of life. And it is Christ who has led us in hope. He faced the challenges of human life, of opposition to his saving mission, of immense suffering and a cruel death. He faced them in hope that God would answer death with resurrection, and answer our sin with newness of life.

Yet it is true that we can hope for more than what Christ hoped for. Not that these are things that Jesus never knew or had not experienced. For him to inspire hope within us, our Saviour needed to experience and to know realities he himself never had to hope for. He never hoped for them because he always enjoyed them for our sake, so that we might be blessed by him with hope to share his joy. Pope Francis says, 'If we consider the way Christ spoke of the Father, we can grasp the love and affection that his human heart felt for him, this complete and constant orientation towards him.'

Jesus never lost sight of his Father. He burst forth with joy in the Holy Spirit: 'No one knows the Father except the Son and those to whom the Son reveals him.' Jesus did not have to hope to get to know the Father or get to know him better. His mind and his heart were bursting with the knowledge and the love of the Father. Through this most intimate knowledge, an immense love that cannot be bettered led Jesus to die for each one of us. Even when he prayed the Psalm on the Cross, 'My God, my God, why have you forsaken me?', every thought of his heart was trained on the Father and our salvation.

Jesus never experienced hope to know or love God better, as though that might await him as a reward. Instead, all his hope was focused on the Father's will. As Pope Francis says, 'When the Son became human, all the hopes and aspirations of his human heart were directed towards the Father.' And so we can hope to share one day in Christ's loving knowledge of the Father and see him face to face with the joy of Christ. As we celebrate the jubilee, we continue to walk by faith and in hope for a fuller share in his joy.

Fr Simon Francis Gaine OP, Dominican teaches theology at the Pontifical University of St Thomas, Rome, and is a member of the International Theological Commission.

Canon Philip Gillespie

As We Wait in Joyful Hope.......

Just outside Liverpool, there are the buildings of the former Seminary of Saint Joseph at Upholland. As a Seminary, it closed in the 1980s but the final decision to close and sell the buildings was taken in 1996. The College Motto was words taken from Psalm 30(31), and then repeated at the conclusion of the great prayer of Thanksgiving, the Te Deum - *'In te domine speravi'* - in you O Lord have I placed my hope.

Although I was never a student at Upholland, its significance in the Diocese was so great that the motto and tradition of the Josephians, i.e. those who studied at Saint Joseph's College, was a living part of my early years as a seminarian. Indeed, I recall that as a Curate, the Parish Priest in Warrington had an Upholland Crest prominently displayed.

A close cousin of hope is trust and that wider sense of being at home with and comfortable in the presence of the Lord. It is all about embracing that vision of your own individual life and journey and the wider story and unfolding of the life of the Church in the world which is God's vision so that the words ' Lord, that I may see' are almost the prayer of each day; Lord that I may have the vision, the perspective of the Gospel in the encounters, the joys and the challenges of my life today.

The trust that we place in the providence and direction which the Lord imparts to our lives is fundamental for our daily living – just as it was obviously foundational for the establishment of Upholland in 1880. In that sense our hope which is placed in the ongoing guidance and inspiration of the Lord, through the gift of the Holy Spirit, is the grace of seeing everything in the perspective of God's will and plan; we do what we can when we can – and we do so joyfully and with confidence.

The Liturgical prayer that we use each day before receiving Communion is for me a significant request but also an act of hope and trust.

Deliver us Lord we pray from every evil, graciously grant peace in our days that, by the help of your mercy, we may be always free from sin and safe from all distress as we await the ***blessed hope*** *and the coming of our Saviour, Jesus Christ.*

It is a 'blessed' hope, which in the previous translation of the Missal said was a 'joyful' hope – and my experience, despite the difficulties and the struggles from which none of us are exempt in our lives, blessed and joyful go hand in hand; it is a joy in the depths of who we are, knowing that we are loved and cherished and supported by the Lord each day – and this knowledge not only frees us from fear and anxiety but it transforms us into people who are free to love and serve those into whose lives we are sent.

Since Ordination I have spent 18 years in the role of a Formator in a Seminary – 8 years at Saint Cuthbert's College Ushaw and now 10 years at Saint Bede's College, Rome, the Beda. I have been immensely fortunate to live amongst people of great hope and trust, both fellow Formation Teams and the Seminarian community. When people have said that it must be lovely living here in Rome amongst such Beauty

I happily concur; Italy is indeed a beautiful place to live in, but far more beautiful is to see someone flourish and grow as they embrace the call of the Lord to the Ordained Ministry in and for the Church and to let their joyful hope deepen and become firmly established. In the task of bringing the good news to others we remember the words often attributed to Saint Francis of Assisi – 'Go, preach the Gospel! And if necessary, use words!'

For a period of time, I was Parish Priest of Saint Mary of the Isle at Douglas on the Isle of Man. In Douglas Bay there is an outcrop of rock which is known as Conister Rock (or Saint Mary's Isle). When Sir William Hillary moved to the Isle of Man in 1808 and saw firsthand the perils of the notoriously choppy Irish Sea he established a boat service which could go the rescue of ships in danger and save lives. This led to the founding of what we now know as the Royal National Lifeboat Institution (RNLI). Eventually he realized that if a ship was in danger it was too far for the crew to immediately swim to the coast at Douglas so he organized the construction of a small refuge facility on Conister rock which was always provided with fresh water and bread, ready to offer shelter from the weather and the sea.

In this way The Tower of Refuge became a visible example of the preparation that Hillary and the people of Douglas wanted to give as a sign of hope for those who were in danger. I think it is a powerful symbol of the ways in which we need not only to wish people well but also make practical preparations to give expression to the hope and refuge offered through the Gospel message; it is almost an example of what John refers to as making our love, our vision and perspective on life something 'real and active' (1 Jn 3:18 NRSV) or, as we will now hear in the Lectionary in the English Standard Version

let us not love in word or talk but indeed and in truth.

At my Ordination one of the hymns which we sang was the well-known and well-loved paraphrase of the Te Deum, written in 1771 by the German Catholic priest Ignaz Franz and translated into English by Clarence A. Walworth in 1858, ***Holy God we praise thy name.***

Spare thy people Lord we pray by a thousand snares surrounded.
Keep us without sin today – never let us be confounded.
Lo I put my hope in thee; never, Lord, abandon me.

May your love be upon us O lord, for we have placed all our hope in you.

Canon Philip Gillespie, Rector of the Pontifical Beda College, Rome

Sir Stephen Hough

He Just Won't Let Go!

I will leave the theologians to define hope as a Theological Virtue from Scripture and Tradition - how it might be fenced in and picked apart. But it struck me that amongst that trinity of virtues (Faith, Hope and Charity) the second is by far the most neglected and misunderstood. Faith and Love are the great pillars of the Temple, the head and heart of Christian spirituality. But hope seems more nebulous, harder to grasp, less 'important'. Like the Holy Spirit in that more famous Trinity, one is tempted to think that it is almost redundant and could perfectly well be covered in its actions by the other Two. It's hard to know what makes it unique or distinctive.

In the famous prayer attributed to Saint Francis d'Assisi, there are two pertinent clauses:

Where there is doubt let me bring faith;
Where there is despair let me bring hope.

Doubt has something of questioning about it, as if articulating a problem which might have a rational solution, something which could be overcome with discourse. Despair is much darker. It goes beyond words to the depths of a person's soul. Its healing can only come from a complete empathy, a com-passionate sharing to the very dregs. "I have doubts" can be comfortably dealt with, Catechism to hand; "I'm in despair" requires a whole different level of engagement.

Faith suggests something solid – a belief that flicking on a certain switch will make the lightbulb glow. But hope is rather more tentative and fluid: that a room dark for decades might come back to life and light again. Hope is in fact all about the 'supernatural', as in the norms of everyday fragile human life being superseded, subverted and challenged. That room of broken illumination, that heart hardened with hatred … perhaps there is a way through. Saint Paul says that "the greatest of these is Love" (1 Cor 13:13), but Someone more authoritative than him has said that whatever we do to the least of his brothers and sisters we do to Him (Mt 25:40). In such acts of mercy, we plant hope as a seed into hearts possibly not yet capable of love.

Hope in God

"If you, O Lord, should mark our guilt, Lord, who would survive?" (Ps 130:3)

We may believe in the forgiveness of God for wrongdoing. That's faith, something we are bound as Christians to affirm. But hope personalizes it. It moves from assent to trust. It's my sins which are forgiven – yes, *that* sin, and *that* sin. It humanizes a doctrine, as Jesus humanizes Divinity. To have faith in God might seem beyond our strength ("prove it!"), but hope is a smaller, more tentative voice. Our ticket to Heaven might be out of date or invalid, but we keep it in our pocket anyway ... in hope.

Hope in others

Faith in others appears to build on something already there; it has a kind of breezy assurance about it. "I've seen what you can do and I'm confident you can do it again, and more." Hope in others begins work when there is no sign of potential, providing the very energy to effect the change needed. It approaches a situation of desperation or despair and begins, kindly and gently, to bring healing. It is there when a parent or teacher instructs a bored or stubborn child; it is there when someone visits a hospital or prison.

Hope in ourselves

Any meaningful hope in ourselves needs to include at least one of the two previous categories: God and others. If I am the only 'I' in which I have hope then the universe has shrunk, and the bar has truly been lowered ... to the ground. But we were born to fly. Or rather, we were born to dream to fly, kept always in anticipation, longing for something we can't quite do which forces us into the arms of the One who can - and who has done already. This is hope. We are lifted high to the extent that we accept that we are earth, we are dust. And this is not just a theological, religious observation. To dream without frustration is the vocation of every human being, believer or not. It is the hope that drives all of us, from our first arm reaching outside the womb, to the final folding of our hands on our chest in the rest of death. I believe that what we hope for deep in our hearts has already been given to us. To be alive is to be chosen. Our recognition of and gratitude for this increases the joy, but it is not the condition for its possession. God is the great Possessor. Of us. And he just won't let go!

Sir Stephen Hough, pianist, composer and writer

Bishop Graham James

A Pilgrim of Hope

"I hope you are well." That's sometimes the first sentence in emails, including from people I scarcely know. I was taught at primary school that it was an appropriate way to begin a letter, although it now seems an anodyne use of the word "hope". "Hope" is used frequently in English to express low grade expectations. "I hope I may get there…" is what we say of an event we have little desire to attend. Such use of "hope" empties the word of any spiritual power. I'm not a good enough linguist to know whether this is a common issue in languages other than English. But, at least for the English-speaking world, the designation by Pope Francis of 2025 as a Year of Hope, when we are encouraged to be "pilgrims of hope", offers a wonderful opportunity to recast hope as one of the great theological virtues.

I've met many "pilgrims of hope" in my life, many of them endowed with such humility that they have not recognized their spiritual authority. Now in my eighth decade, my mind returns to how I was formed in the Christian faith in my early years. The Christian faith was part of the air I breathed in my family, but one grandparent seemed to inhabit a universe of hope, despite having only the most basic education and experiencing many limitations. She lived and breathed the presence of God. Expectation was written all over her face. This "pilgrim of hope" was my maternal grandmother, Edith.

She was widowed when only in her late forties. Even into the 1960s Edith's small, rented Cornish cottage had no indoor toilet, with water coming only from a tap outside the back door. She became blind as a result of glaucoma shortly before I was born. She suffered such psychological torment that she spent several months in a mental hospital, although in those days she was not offered any helpful therapy. It felt like a further punishment. Somehow, she recovered – no one knew how – and her Methodist faith was renewed. My memory of her was that she was always smiling. Whenever I hear the words "beatific vision" I see her in my mind's eye. She lived in reduced circumstances and gradually became deaf too but radiated grace, a companion of hope. The only theological statement she was inclined to repeat was "God is good". Somehow, she lived in connection with the source of love at the heart of the universe, whom we call God for shorthand, revealed in Jesus Christ. She was devoid of ambitions for herself, accepting the world around her. She seemed to see beauty in people and the world around her more profoundly than the sighted and more privileged. She died when I was fourteen, but I now realize she influenced my life and vocation profoundly.

What I learned instinctively from her was that life's negative experiences could be redeemed. Her blindness seemed to have sensitized her more deeply. She lived in a community which thrived on gossip and was parochially minded, yet I never heard her speak uncharitably about anyone. The transformative power of the God of hope in her life gave her hope for others. However, she did not look forward optimistically to a better future in this life and expected no favours in the next beyond being with God himself and enfolded in the divine love. That's what made her such an authentic pilgrim of hope. We need more of them, witnessing to hope in Christ without consciously attempting to influence anyone, lights on the path and signposts on the Way.

When hope is weak, gloom takes over and gradually turns into fear. In 2023 a report on the Mental Health of Children and Young People in England recorded that over 20% of 8 to 25 year-olds had a probable mental health disorder. It's a shocking figure. But that report did not address this as a spiritual problem. When we ignore spiritual dis-ease, it adds to our fears. Fear envelops all our sensibilities quickly, and the world seems bleak.

There's an old story about two rabbis who, after a long debate about the fundamentals of religion, came to the conclusion that God did not exist. The next morning one of the rabbis saw the other praying. He was astonished and said to his friend he thought they'd agreed God did not exist. "What's that got to do with it?" answered the praying rabbi. I've seen this story used to illustrate widely different points – that religious beliefs and religious practice are entirely different, or that prayer is a habit without meaning. The story speaks to me of the way people frequently pray when they cannot explain to whom they are praying or are not even certain as to whether there is a God to hear them at all. The instinct to pray, which seems almost universal in the human condition, is a sign of a deep hope within us to be in relationship with the power of love that inhabits and animates our world. The mind can be convinced that there is no God; the heart is less easy to influence by argument. We are not usually argued into love. We discover love. And, I believe, we discover hope too, sometimes through the most negative of experiences, as with my grandmother Edith. That hope deep within us is also the hope at the heart of the universe. It's why we are called to be "pilgrims of hope".

The Rt Revd Graham James is a former Bishop of Norwich in the Church of England, and in retirement continues to minister in the Diocese of Truro

Alderman Vincent Keaveny

The Presence of Hope

Inspiration, like hope, comes in many guises. I often turn to that wickedly humorous masterwork of the American journalist, Ambrose Bierce, The Devil's Dictionary (1906). Bierce defines hope as 'desire and expectation rolled into one'. He goes on to illustrate this with a few lines of poetry written by one of his alter egos, 'Fogarty Weffing':

'Delicious Hope! when naught to man is left
Of fortune destitute, of friends bereft,
When even his dog deserts him...
Then [Hope]....
Descendent, radiant from the skies to hint
The promise of a clerkship in the Mint.'

Bierce's cynical sense of hope's meaning and limitations is something many of us have shared on occasion. We want, we need, something, so we allow an expectation to form in our minds, however unlikely the fulfilment of that expectation might be. Sometimes chance does intervene and an unreasonable hope is fulfilled. It may take a number of rollovers but the lottery will be won. For almost everyone with a ticket in their hand on a Saturday night, however, the hint of a promise of a lottery funded future slips away, until next week.

I prefer the view of hope as a positive force in our lives, an essential feature of our human nature and our relationship with God. Emily Dickinson's poem, 'Hope is the Thing with Feathers' (c. 1861) brings this to life. She writes:

"Hope" is the thing with feathers -
That perches in the soul -
And sings the tune without the words -
And never stops - at all"

The metaphor of hope as an ever-singing bird at the heart of our soul has biblical resonances, with a contemporary echo in the songs of Leonard Cohen. We may choose not to listen or to hear but the song of hope is constant, even in the most challenging of moments.

I had the privilege of serving as the Lord Mayor of London in 2021/22 as the world emerged from lockdowns, facemasks and Covid tests. It was a time of hope: people were starting to travel again and to meet family and friends with a confidence that took many of them by surprise. I hosted the Lord Mayor's Banquet in Guildhall, at the heart of the City of London, in November 2021 at the start of my year in office. We had 680 guests in Greathall that night, most of whom had not been in a room with more than a handful of others for 18 months or more. It was a very odd but hopeful occasion as we relearned social arts and conventions that some thought might never return.

My Mayoral theme for the year - 'People and Purpose' - captured that sense of hope too. A focus on making the most of diverse talent, driving social mobility, encouraging investment with positive social impact and taking practical steps to finance the transition to net zero in the face of climate change. Another rewarding and reliable source of inspiration, Dr Johnson's Dictionary (1755), provides four definitions of hope. Each is valuable: an 'expectation of some good'; 'confidence in a future event'; 'that which gives hope, that on which hopes are fixed'; and 'the object of hope'. In my Mayoral year I saw the power of hope as reflected in those definitions at work.

In May 2022 I convened the City of London's first Net Zero Delivery Summit bringing together international leaders in the climate change arena, such as John Kerry and Mark Carney, with representatives of global banks, asset management and insurance companies. That 'expectation of some good' ran through the discussions of the two days of the meeting. Dr Johnson cites the words of Job, that seem so appropriate: '*There is hope of a tree, if cut down, that it will sprout again*' (Job, xiv 7). As the global political landscape changes again, and the international resolve to tackle climate change is weakened, we need to remember Job's words and the hope that inspired those discussions in Mansion House in 2022.

Later that month, I launched Progress Together, a membership body promoting greater socio-economic diversity in the financial services industry. Progress Together emerged from the work of a taskforce commissioned by the UK Government that I co-chaired. The taskforce identified the scale of the challenge facing the financial services sector in retaining and promoting to senior positions employees from a lower socio-economic background. Today we have 56 member firms, with a third of the UK financial services workforce represented in our membership. As those firms and their employees take steps to change the sector for the better, I see the hope that Dr Johnson categorizes as 'confidence in a future event'. Hope galvanizes and inspires those looking to effect that change. It is the tune without the words we hear in our hearts.

Emily Dickinson ends her poem with this stanza:

'I've heard it in the chillest land -
And on the strangest Sea -
Yet - never - in Extremity,
It asked a crumb - of me.'

Hope, she writes, is present even in the most difficult situations. The song is always to be heard if we listen for it. It asks nothing of us. We do not need to analyse or unpack it, or to seek to enhance its utility in some way. Hope is that feathered thing whose song is at the centre of our human experience and draws us to God and the life beyond this one.

Alderman Vincent Keaveny CBE, Lord Mayor of London 2021/22

Fr Toby Lees, OP

Resurrection Hope

One Sunday in November, more wintry than autumnal, I set out with a couple of my Dominican brothers and some parishioners to bless the graves of our departed parishioners up at the local cemetery. Other parishioners join us, making their own way there, and each goes and stands by the graves of their loved ones, waiting for one of the priests to come and pray with them and bless the grave.

It's a sombre time all round, but there is a particular sadness as you approach the infant area of the cemetery. All death is unnatural, but headstones here - many bigger than those whose graves they mark - are markers of deaths that go outside the order of death to which we have become accustomed. This is a place of real sorrow, a place of enduring pain.

As I had finished blessing the grave of one child who never managed to take a breath outside his mother's womb, I saw another lady a few metres away, not one of our regular parishioners. She was sitting quietly in a camping chair, no phone, no flask, no book, no blanket, and it was cold. I walked over and asked if she would like the grave blessed and she said, 'Yes,' and told me that this was Baby Zion, this was her son. I blessed the grave and hugged the mother, and then she resumed her lonely vigil at the side of her child's grave.

What was she expecting, why was she waiting? To some her vigil would be an act of futility, she should move on. To me it was a painful act of love, and, whether she knew it or not, I think she was waiting for what Tolkien would call a eucatastrophe and of which the Resurrection was the greatest example.

November, for Catholics, is a month with a focus on the dead, but it is not a macabre focus, it is one made bearable by present hope for a different future, made possible by a past event: the Resurrection! The joy and power of the Resurrection which reverberates throughout all time, all creation, enables us to live with the reality of the many Good Fridays that life in a fallen world brings, confident that the redemptive power of the Cross enters into our suffering and gives it meaning and that the Resurrection promises new life and the wiping away of every tear.

On a purely human level it would be easy as a priest to give way to despair. On the purely human level life can sometimes seem more Good Friday than Easter Sunday. And, yet - and I hope this is your experience too – most priests are not sad. They love their vocation. Why?

It is not because we feel tremendously successful. Or, at least I don't. For every person I help to receive into the Church how many leave? For every young person's imagination I manage to somehow capture, how many more are bored? And this is not false humility, children have little guile and I have seen the yawns, restlessness, and evident desire to be anywhere but here when I've been giving a talk in a school! Most of you will have at least one family member for whom the faith is no longer something living and your efforts with them may seem to come to nothing.

Sometimes it feels like you win the odd skirmish, but the defeats keep on mounting up. I know I'm not alone in this. It's a sentiment that Tolkien shared when he wrote: *Actually I am a Christian, and indeed a Roman Catholic, so that I do not expect 'history' to be anything but a 'long defeat' - though it contains (and in a legend may contain more clearly and movingly) some samples or glimpses of final victory.*

But what Tolkien had, what I have, what I suspect that lady at the graveside had, or, rather, what we have received is hope. A hope that is not simply that of an optimistic temperament, but a hope which is theological, a gift of God.

For many the hope we have is that of a child who has not outgrown a fairy story. People like Dawkins often dismiss faith and our hope as belief in fairies. So be it. But fairy stories will outlast the works of Dawkins, and Tolkien thought them mightily important, because he thought them, in their most essential elements, true.

Tolkien said that there are three functions of a fairy story: recovery, escape, and consolation. In recovery we are made to see clearly once more, the grime is removed from the windows of our ordinary experience of the world. In escape there is a flight into the secondary world, but this is not the escapism which characterizes so much modern entertainment. We might think of it as an entry into another world, but one which contains the same moral structure and essential cosmic dimensions as our own, and so is a training of the imagination to see the 'real world' more clearly when we come back to it. And the consolation – the eucatastrophe - is the happy ending, which the child (whatever their age, be it 4 or 44) knows is coming and yet simultaneously fears might not: the condition of suspense. Consolation, he suggests, is the highest purpose of a fairy story: 'Almost I would venture' he says, 'to assert that all complete fairy-stories must have it... I will call it Eucatastrophe.'

Eucatastrophe is the amazing grace, the rabbit out of the hat moment, the victory from the jaws of defeat, the bursting open of the tomb of a child in a cold, wet cemetery. It is the unforeseen turn for the better when all human hope seems lost.

You see it throughout Tolkien's writings, perhaps most obviously at the moment Frodo's strength fails and he decides to keep the ring for himself. It all looks to be ending in failure . . . and then . . . Gollum suddenly intervenes - Gollum who is only still there because of Frodo's forgiveness time and time again - with malicious intent, but unwittingly saves the day. For as Gollum is in the process of biting off Frodo's finger to claim the ring, he falls into the lava of Mount Doom and destroys the ring.

Tolkien explains that eucatastrophe is not incompatible with 'the existence of "dyscatastrophe", of sorrow and failure: the possibility of these is [in fact] necessary to the joy of deliverance; [the eucatastrophe] denies universal final defeat and in so far is evangelium [good news, the best news in fact], giving a fleeting glimpse of joy, joy beyond the walls of the world, poignant as grief.'

An important part of what Tolkien is getting at here is something Simone Weil saw when she said: 'Love of God is pure when joy and suffering inspire an equal degree of gratitude.' The Resurrection permeates everything. It puts the 'good' in Good Friday; and *good* cannot be contained.

The gospels, for Tolkien, contain the ultimate Eucatastrophe: 'The Birth of Christ is the Eucatastrophe of Man's history. The Resurrection is the Eucatastrophe of the story of the Incarnation. This story begins and ends in joy.'

As I think of that woman sitting in her long vigil by the grave of her son, Baby Zion, a line from Scripture keeps recurring in my head, 'Can these dry bones live?'

And the Resurrection cries out, 'Yes, these dry bones can live!' The Lord can breathe life into these dry bones and into the dead in a London cemetery.

Can these dry bones live? Yes! Does that woman wait in vain at the grave of Baby Zion? No! Can we look at death head on and say with Saint Paul, 'Death, where is thy sting?' Yes, we can! Has Christ Risen from the dead and in doing so opened up the way for us to eternal life? Even in our suffering, there is hope.

This essay is adapted from an essay which first appeared in Magnificat British Edition and is reproduced with kind permission.

Fr Toby Lees OP. Assistant Priest Saint Dominic's Haverstock Hill and Director of Radio Maria

Bishop Jane Mainwaring

Trusting in Hope

I'm usually a glass half full type of person with an optimistic outlook on life. A majority of the time that comes naturally but other times it is a conscious choice to choose to believe in something better to come, to give people the benefit of the doubt, to choose hope over despair, to see the good rather than the bad. This is partly due to personality, but it's also rooted in over 40 years of trusting in the goodness and faithfulness of God and of seeing that trust justified time and time again.

There is only one time in my life where I have been very conscious of feeling like I'd lost all hope in a situation. I had been grappling with a very long and difficult family situation and after months of trying to stay positive through the ups and downs of the situation there was a moment when I felt that there was no hope. I can still see in my mind's eye exactly where I was when I admitted that I'd lost hope. I couldn't see how this situation was ever going to end well.

Years on from that time, I look back and can recall the words of others around me during that period. Some added to the sense of fear and despair. Others tried to offer words of hope and encouragement. In that moment it was easier to accept the words of pessimism which played into my own despondency than it was to accept the words of hope.

As I look back I think hope, even in the worst of days, actually didn't come in the words which people spoke but in the many acts of kindness I received from those around me from practical support, to allowing me to carry on working by gently taking enough off my plate to make that possible, to keeping in contact through the long months of struggle, to the forgiveness I received when I wasn't at my best, to people being willing to travel the journey with me however hard and for ever long.

In the end, hope was rewarded and my worst fears didn't materialize. But that time had a profound impact on me and was a time when my belief in the God who brings light into the darkness was tested. It was difficult to see that light for a time.

As I marked Good Friday that year, the profound pain and the seeming hopelessness of the crucifixion spoke to me in a way that I've never experienced before. It felt like I was stuck in the pain of the cross unable to see the light and hope that the resurrection would bring.

Reflecting on that time since, I am reminded of a verse from the hymn 'Brother, sister, let me serve you'. The verse reads *'I will hold the Christ light for you in the night time of your fear; I will hold my hand out to you, speak the peace you long to hear'.*

I will never forget the hope that was demonstrated through the kind actions of those around me when my ability to be hopeful was drained. To me they held the Christ light for me when all I could see was the darkness. They physically, emotionally and spiritually held their hands out to me. Even though God seemed absent in the hopelessness and my prayers felt unheard and unanswered, through the actions of others God still offered his hope even when I couldn't see it or receive it.

I recall another time, in my first year of being of a priest where I can still see in my mind's eye exactly where I was. I was standing in a parishioner's kitchen, having just prayed with their elderly father who was bed bound and close to death, watching the second plane hit the Twin Towers in New York on what was to become known as 9/11.

That following Sunday I was due to preach at the main service in church. It was one of those occasions where the single and most important task I had was to help people understand the question of where God was in the midst of so much destruction, pain and death.

The passage I preached on was just one verse: *And now faith, hope and love abide, these three; and the greatest of these is love* (1 Cor 13:13).

Despite all that had happened just 6 days before, my response on that day was to gently say even so, faith, hope and love abide. God was in the midst of the pain and in the midst of the despair. He was in the broken bodies and the lives torn apart. He was in the grief and the separation from loved ones because he knew that searing and desperate pain as his own Son hung on the cross.

But as much as God was in the pain, he was in the resurrection too. Sometimes the hope of the resurrection can feel out of reach and sometimes the darkness can be all consuming, but I hope that on that Sunday morning I was able to hold the Christ light for others as others would, years later, do the same for me.

The Rt Revd Dr Jane Mainwaring
Bishop of Hertford

Revd Rob Marshall

An Open Spirit, a Trusting Heart and a Far-Sighted Vision

Hope has been one of the fundamental themes of much of Pope Francis' public utterances and writings throughout his Pontificate.

So, it is no surprise that he has encouraged the faithful in the Holy Year of 2025 to explore more deeply how we define hope and how we cannot lose sight of it in an increasingly turbulent world.

During 2024 I have been celebrating a personal anniversary. It is 40 years since I was ordained priest at the age of just 23 in Ripon Cathedral, North Yorkshire.

Over the past 40 years there have been many moments of pure joy. Plenty of moments too when I have wondered what will follow next. There have been times of exhilaration, tiredness, tears and joy. Momentous events which have shaken the world have suddenly sprung up as the backdrop to the year.

The myriad of pastoral occasions and opportunities for ministry as priest against a fluid background of universal uncertainty has demanded that I keep hope to the very front of my prayers at all times however challenging the situation.

It is the wonder of the Daily Office which has sustained me most through these decades of ministry. As priest I join each day with others in saying prayers and reading scripture. And there it is - undoubtedly and outstandingly in the Book of Psalms - that the transforming power of God's hope consistently communicates itself to those who are pausing and praying.

The 150 Psalms contained in the Psalter reflect a variety of genres. Prayers of lament and thanksgiving, hymns, cries of sorrow and appeals for deliverance. The Psalms are the pilgrim's prayer & hymn book in which hope rather than being a mere concept is an experienced reality. Hope is something we always have (71:14) because God never forsakes us (23:4) because he is our shield, and we put our hope always in God's word (119:114).

Whatever is going on in the world, or in parish ministry, or with family and friends, these kinds of verses jump out at you daily. Because and through God's grace we come to know that it is never as bad or as impossible as it may seem as long as we cling on faithfully to our hope in God. My favourite verse of this genre is Psalm 42:5: "Why my soul, are you downcast? Who is so disturbed with me? Put your hope in God, for I will yet praise Him, my Saviour and My God."

The Psalmist asks a straightforward question with which we can all identify when we feel hopeless: "Why God?" But here the author is asking the question of his soul – the Hebrew word being nephesh – which can mean the breath or spirit that gives us life. So the question, soliloquy style, is *why is this innermost part of me cast down, lifeless and disquieted within me?* We are praying when reading this Psalm – *hey Lord what's going on, I do not want to lose sight of the hope God promises me daily* – before rallying and remembering *for yet I shall praise Him for the help of His countenance.* The God of hope is always there whenever I need him, even in those moments when I forget him even for a short time.

When announcing the 2025 Jubilee Pope Francis wrote: "We must fan the flame of hope that has been given us and help everyone to gain new strength and certainty by looking to the future with an open spirit, a trusting heart and far-sighted vision." There are three boxes there to tick in the Holy Year in terms of hope. Open Spirit? Trusting Heart? Far sighted Vision?

Looking back on my own ministry in terms of both parish life and in the media as a broadcaster on BBC radio over many years, holding on to hope is obviously key. In our journeys with fellow pilgrims, it is a daily task to fan the flames of hope as Pope Francis urges us to do. With the world in the state that it is, with increased political and diplomatic uncertainty, which is unlike anything I can ever remember during my years as a priest, this is a huge calling for each pilgrim.

I have presented *Thought for the Day* on BBC Radio 4 in the Uk for almost twenty years. Part of a team of broadcasters we are asked to give "a little bit of poetry" by reflecting on the day's news for just under 3 minutes to an audience of several million. Every time I start to write a script I am confronted with a blank screen and pray hard that somehow in the context of the morass of worldly events I can find something which ticks at least one of the boxes marked hope.

One example of this was a recent contact I have had with Sister Telesphora Pavlou and the Community of Franciscan Sisters on the Mount of Beatitudes in northern Galilee. They are not far from the Lebanese border where rockets have been landing for months. I reached out to her because I heard that the site, so long associated with Jesus' Sermon on the Mount and the Beatitudes had been under physical attack.

Sister Telesphora ticked all the "hope boxes" in a real-life highly dangerous situation which many of us would have found impossible. Every word of her testimony fanned the flames of hope: *Our area is now subject to more intensive continuous attacks. We remain strong in faith and only our sisters remain here; no one else is left. Our Triune and One God is protecting us even if we have had many fires because of the explosions in the fields around us.*"

She and her fellow Sisters have been an inspiration to all of us in the parish following in a long line of courageous Christians who embrace and spread a spirit of hope to others without thought for self.

The Jubilee gives us an opportunity to be courageous too. To broadcast the essence of the hope Jesus offers as we face up to an uncertain future. Our spirits need to be truly open, our hearts to be truly trusting, our eyes looking far into the distance to a vision of God's glory and the transfiguration of hope into everlasting joy.

The Revd Canon Dr Rob Marshall
Rector of Digswell, writer and broadcaster

Fr Stephen Morrison, O. Praem

Peregrinantes in Spem

Firstly, a little grammar exercise. When I first heard of the theme for the Holy Year 2025, I leapt with my usual pedantic enthusiasm to see how the official Latin version – normally the international one upon which other translations are based – was worded. It will be of interest to the faithful, and not merely to scholars, to explain the "*in + accusative*" structure of the last phrase. Since the phrase is translated into English as "Pilgrims *of* hope," one might have supposed, given the possessive in English, that a genitive (*spei*) might have appeared in the Latin, but no! Nor is it the "*in + ablative*" structure (which, since it might imply "inside" would have been a little odd); nor even is it a simple ablative of instrument (*spe*) which might have also been confusing: after all, we are not pilgrims *by* or *with* hope, unless the meaning is that hope is how we journey on our pilgrimage, which in itself might bear thinking about. Rather, we have a structure common to Ecclesiastical Latin, "in" followed by an accusative noun, which always implies *motion towards* something. In other words, we are pilgrims "into" hope, or pilgrims "towards" hope. Perhaps the image is that we are not merely "hopeful pilgrims" – we are journeying *towards 'hope'* as the goal, or end of our pilgrimage. Clearly, our hopes are only fulfilled in God; hence, we might draw a parallel with the use of the same structure in the Latin version of the Creed: "Credo *in unum*

Deum" – which implies not only believing in God (i.e., that he exists), but that our faith takes us somehow *into* God; belief is a *motion towards* God. So, in this jubilee year, our pilgrimage is one *towards hope.*

Naturally, I do not argue with the official translation into English, "Pilgrims of Hope." In fact, most European languages have done the same thing. But the designers of the logo were keen to point out that there is a dynamic quality to this jubilee pilgrimage – it is *going* somewhere. We are not idly talking about "being on a journey;" we really are headed towards the Cross, towards Christ, towards the one whose birth is the entire point of our Jubilee, marking another quarter-century after two thousand years of His incarnation. I once heard a French bishop preaching about his diocese being "en marche" – that is, walking on a journey – which implies also that the Church is alive (the opposite of "en marche" – working – would be "en panne" – broken down!). However, the preacher admitted, exactly where we are going is a mystery: "nous ne savons pas où nous allons." This struck me as both profound but meaningless, if that's possible, at the same time; either it means that the aim of our journey, God, is the profoundest of all mysteries – which is undoubtedly true – or it means that the Church is blindly wandering like the people of Israel in the desert, following the pillars of fire and cloud without really knowing if, let alone when, they are to enter the Promised Land. Perhaps I have just given more meaning to the phrase I so glibly thought meaningless at first hearing; but it shows how we ought to be careful to be precise about what the "pilgrim Church on earth" is really doing in its "motion towards" God. One assumes that the bishop wanted to ask that question sincerely: where was his diocese really headed? Towards God, one hopes.

The Rule of Saint Augustine calls its followers to be "of one heart and one soul on the way to God." The Latin has the same construction as the phrase we are meditating upon: "in Deum." A community of Augustinian brothers or sisters is therefore called to be unanimous on their journey "into God." Thus it is not merely a description of the religious life, or of the Christian life, as a voyage towards the Creator; it is also an invitation to contemplation, to take the plunge as it were, to dive into God through contemplative prayer and community life. Perhaps our Jubilee theme is an invitation to do the same: let us plunge into the mystery of HOPE, and see where it takes us. We can trust it; as Saint Paul says, "Hope is not deceptive" (Rom 5:5), meaning that it does not disappoint us, because it will be the fulfilment of all our longings. What we speak of in human terms as our "hopes and dreams" will be fulfilled in the One who is our Hope.

The Liturgy is very clear on this, when, in conclusion of the Lord's Prayer, we ask our Heavenly Father to deliver us from all evil and from all distress, while "we await the Blessed Hope, and the coming of our Saviour Jesus Christ." This is of course drawn from Saint Paul's Letter to Titus (2:13) in which it is the *appearing*, or the *coming*, of the "glory of our great God and Saviour Jesus Christ" which is the hope itself. We might summarize it by saying that Paul is teaching us that Jesus, at his Second Coming, is the blessed Hope we are waiting for. So, in this jubilee year, we are journeying and making a pilgrimage *into* Hope, towards Christ.

What helps me in my faith, not only as a priest but firstly as a Christian, is the fact that God's revelation of Himself to humankind is clear that I can have a "sure and certain hope of the resurrection" – a phrase, in fact, used at Journey's End, during the burial service. In other words, my hope is not merely a wish, or a desire, springing from myself; it is the result of God's message of Salvation to all of us. We have hope because Christ has become our Hope; He is my hope. I need not worry about not knowing everything there is to know about heaven, my final destination: the fact that it is a mystery ought not to diminish my hope. Rather, firm in my convictions that Christ is the Way, the Truth and the Life, I take up my own pilgrim journey in certain knowledge that He will lead me to Himself, and be Himself the object of my hope. My job now, meanwhile, is to proclaim that hope to everyone else, especially to those most tempted by despair, which is a lack of hope. As Saint Peter wrote to those undergoing persecutions for the Faith, "make a defence to anyone who calls you to account for the hope that is in you." Christ, my Hope, is the object of my journey; my pilgrimage is one *into* Him, not just towards Him, but the glorious truth is that He is there, in my heart – "the hope that is *in* you." That, after all, was Augustine's great intuition – while he was searching for God in all kinds of wrong places, he eventually found Him within his own soul. I pray that during this jubilee, we will find that very hope springing eternal from within us, as we realize that we are also travelling towards Him who is our Blessed Hope. At least, I hope so.

Fr Stephen Morrison O Praem – Priory of Our Lady of Sorrows, Peckham

Canon John O'Leary

We Live in Hope

Vivamus in Spe, "Let us live in hope": the motto of Allen Hall Seminary. It is a most fitting motto. Formation for priesthood is a call to live in hope. Hope must be woven into all we do and are.

Without hope, knowing my sinfulness and fragility, I would crumble before the mission, with all its challenges, entrusted to me as Rector: that is, to accompany seminarians in the adventure of becoming fully conformed to Christ, the High Priest. Through entering into communion with the charity of the Good Shepherd, their hearts, my heart, must be transformed into the image of the heart of Christ.

What, though, is the hope, in which I, the seminarians, you, we are called to live? We hope for all manner of things, small and great. I hope West Ham will win the Premiership. We hope warfare will end. These hopes have their place and value. Above all, however, we are to live in the greatest hope: the hope implanted in us as God's gracious gift when we were baptized. This is the hope the Father gives us as his beloved children; the hope that keeps us turned toward the Father in loving, childlike trust. It is the hope inflamed and sustained by the Holy Spirit. It is the hope whose substance is faith in Christ's death, resurrection and ascension. It is the hope that steadily waits for the coming of God's Kingdom already amongst us in Christ. It is the hope that makes present even now Christ's glorious appearance at history's end. Christ is our hope!

Christ, our hope, motivates us to set forth on our pilgrimage towards the everlasting life for which we were created, confident that no matter the tribulations we experience, we shall reach journey's end. Always humble and grateful, our hope is for nothing less than to be enfolded, body and soul, in the Communion of Love, the Most Holy Trinity. Yet hope for so marvellous a future, satisfying the deepest yearning of our hearts, whilst surpassing our natural limits, affords us present joy amidst every trial. It convinces us that in Christ, God is with us every step we take.

As God's gift, hope cannot be exclusive. Hope frees us from self-enclosure. A steadfast anchor, yes; but hope also launches us on a voyage towards others, inspires authentic love for them. It impels us to liberate those imprisoned in any form of despair. Hope for the glorious future Christ opens for us, sends us forth in union with him to suffer with and for others *here and now,* to bring Christ's healing to *this* world. Should I cease seeking to form priests to be heralds of such hope, cease to have such hope myself, then I would cease to be Rector. Thankfully, Allen Hall has a rich treasury of witnesses to keep hope alive.

The seminary stands where once stood Saint Thomas More's Chelsea home. Whilst imprisoned in the Tower of London awaiting execution, he wrote to his daughter, Margaret. The saint readily confesses 'past wickedness'. Nevertheless, he resolutely trusts in the Lord's mercy. He lost goods and land, and would soon lose his life, but still he says: "I will not mistrust him, Meg, though I shall feel myself weakening and on the verge of being overcome with fear". The father comforts his daughter: "He will not let me be lost.

I shall, therefore, with good hope commit myself wholly to him". This hope ignited within Saint Thomas' heart immense charity, including towards those who unjustly condemned him.

Though now in Chelsea, Allen Hall's roots reach back to 1568, to Douai College founded in Flanders by Cardinal William Allen. One hundred and fifty-nine Douai men were martyred for their Catholic Faith. Hope fuelled their mission, even to embracing most tortuous deaths. With these words, Blessed Joseph Lambton encouraged his fellow martyr, Blessed Edward Waterson, on the eve of their execution: "Let us be merry, for tomorrow I hope we shall have a heavenly breakfast".

I have been given another precious witness to hope, my brother Francis. He died aged 26, from leukaemia. For three years he endured aggressive therapies. He received bone marrow transplants twice. Twice the cancer returned. Sometimes he felt very low, though never despaired. When told nothing more could be done, Francis faced imminent death loving this life as long as it lasted whilst not afraid to dic.

The day before his death, Francis told me: "I thank God for my illness because it has taught me the most important things in life: love of friends, love of family, love of God." He admitted, "I've done lots of stupid things, but I don't regret them". Not because he was without contrition, rather, as he explained, "because I trust in Christ as my saviour". From those "stupid things" arose complete abandonment to Christ. Christ, whom Francis met in the sacraments of Reconciliation and Anointing shortly before he died, so too in Holy Communion on the day of his death. Having enjoyed a genuine foretaste of the heavenly banquet, strengthened by the Lord's Body and Blood, Francis set out on the final stage of his pilgrimage to what, I pray with sure hope, was his greatest hope's fulfilment: to share in the very glory of God, of which every Eucharist is the pledge.

When my hope is not so strong as Francis' and the martyrs', I turn to Mary. At the foot of the Cross, sharing like no other in her Son's suffering, Mary's hope never died. Nor was her hope buried by the grief of Holy Saturday. The certitude of hope upheld Mary throughout her patient vigil for the invincible joy of resurrection's dawn. Now assumed into heaven, Mary remains at our side.

Mary, Mother of Hope, bring to birth and nurture in our hearts your Son, Light in the darkest abyss. Pray that we may be radiant presences of him, proclaiming to all who dwell in death's shadow: "Let us live in hope".

Canon Dr John O'Leary, Rector of Allen Hall Seminary, Chelsea, London

Darren Perkes

Hope as Consolation

Like many of you reading these pages, I have often found myself looking through the lens of life darkly, questioning meaning and the purpose of things like suffering and pain. I remember particularly witnessing the sad deterioration of one of my close friends who had motor-neurone disease, a bright and incredibly gifted human being with so much to offer life, declining so quickly and so visibly in front of me. He often turned to me to discuss matters of faith, including his increasing doubt as he moved towards the end of his life. I will never forget when I sat next to him the day before he died, I looked into his eyes (as he could no longer verbally communicate), making some attempt to reassure. He wrote on his iPad, *'I do hope you are right Darren'*. These words have stayed with me, and I think gently guide me into a focus on hope, whatever that means to us.

I count myself very fortunate that I have always had a sense of faith, going back to a very early age when I asked my mother to lift me up as a child, to touch the feet of the crucified Christ outside the church we used to walk past on the way to nursery school. I just 'knew' there was something important represented in the crucified, suffering figure on the cross. That 'knowing' has stayed with me right to this day. I work now as a psychologist with people across varying roles and disciplines in life and it is often this sense of 'knowing' that also comes into my work, like a light guiding me. This Light I believe to be the same sense I felt when I asked to be picked up to connect with the suffering Lord. It is when we are in a place of suffering, that we need light, that we need hope.

Many of you may already be aware that we are imperfect beings, particularly in the way our mind, our brain has evolved. We have evolved to focus more on the negative, to pay attention to those aspects of life that may be threatening or fearful. In my work I use ACT (Acceptance and Commitment Therapy) to help my clients understand and, in many ways, normalize critical and negative thinking with a view to learning to accept, to be at peace with that part of ourselves. ACT also encourages us then to turn towards what is meaningful – our Purpose, our core Values. It is this that I believe summarizes the human condition, we are all caught between suffering and learning to accept suffering with a view to having Hope – a turning towards what is meaningful to us. For me as a Christian, the Source of that Hope is Christ. When my friend said to me *"I do hope you are right'*, I trusted, I had faith and belief that the life of Jesus Christ has conquered death and opened the gate of heaven to bring hope, to bring Light Eternal.

When I can, I usually try to say Morning Prayer as part of my own personal and spiritual development. I often pause when I come to the final lines of the Benedictus:

'He will give light to those in darkness, those who dwell in the shadow of death, and guide us into the way of peace'.

These lines summarize for me the essence of what is hope and particularly what we are asked to do as Christians. If we have faith that Jesus conquered death, that he *truly conquered death* and opened the gate of Heaven to all believers, then we have faith in that Light. That Light when it shines brings hope. *'He will give light to those in darkness'*. If we know that this will happen when He enters our lives, then we must share that hope with others.

In my parish I work in the ministry of consolation, receiving training from the Diocese to comfort those who are grieving. Those who are in a place of pain and loss. It is an immense privilege to be with people who feel safe enough to be open with you to share their darkest pain. This links to what I believe is the greatest gift we can give another – to truly listen to them. What if when we truly listen to others, we help bring Christ into their lives? What if when we truly listen to another, we help them find a sense of comfort, and over time, help then turn towards Him to share their pain? I would ask all of us as Christians to pause and ask ourselves, when did we last truly listen to another? It may be in that listening that we are able to bring Hope to others, helping them turn towards that Light.

I remember recently approaching a priest in my parish here to ask for the Ministry of Reconciliation. I was troubled with areas in my life that were making me feel burdened, overloaded. He gently asked how I was before asking to talk to him, to *'forget the usual formalities'* and just to outline where I was. He listened to me in the deepest way I have not experienced in a long time. He encouraged me by his reflections, to think of small ways I could give back - to daily ask myself what I could do to give back to the Christ child, what he had so wonderfully given to me. He also explained the differing ways we can give back, through prayer, attendance at Mass and through acts of mercy, providing his own examples to illustrate this. He also explained how by our willingness to become so vulnerable in front of another, we are trusting the Lord to work with us. He did this himself, he also become vulnerable in front of me, sharing his own weaknesses to help connect with me.

I walked away from that experience feeling lighter, unburdened. I also had hope. There is no doubt that what he did in this encounter helped me to connect with the Lord. I physically and spiritually sensed His presence in the interaction. That presence was unconditional Love. And this for me is the essence of what the gift of Hope is about, we are helping to *guide others into the way of peace,* and we do this by using the gifts the Lord has given us, trusting in Him to guide and speak through us. This is what I felt instinctively when I said to my friend with Motor-Neurone disease, *'do not be afraid, it will all be OK'*. We are willing to be brave, to point others towards something that we have not seen but can only believe to be true – the Lord of Light, the Lord of Love.

There is a wonderful quote from Saint Paul I refer to frequently, to remind myself of what we are called to do as Christians, as believers in the Lord of Light, the Lord of Love:

'Blessed be the God and Father of our Lord Jesus Christ, a gentle Father and the God of all consolation, who comforts us in all our sorrows, so that we can offer others, in their sorrows, the consolation that we have received from God ourselves. Indeed, as the sufferings of Christ overflow to us, so through Christ does our consolation overflow'.

Reflect on this if you can, read it slowly, allowing its meaning to flow into the essence of who you are. We have received such consolation from God, such hope that He asks us to share this with others. Look at the words of how the sufferings of Christ overflow to us and through us, we allow that consolation to overflow to others. This is what we believe as Christians we are called to do – to offer Light, Hope, Consolation to all those with us who are walking alongside us. Try the gentle listening if you can, allow the Lord to work through you, to bring his gentle Love and guidance to others.

Darren Perks

Parishioner Saint John's, Horsham

Fr Dominic Robinson, S.J.

Trustworthy Hope

'Redemption is offered to us in the sense that we have been given hope, trustworthy hope, by virtue of which we can face our present: the present, even if it is arduous, can be lived and accepted if it leads towards a goal, if we can be sure of this goal, and if this goal is great enough to justify the effort of the journey' (*Spe Salvi,* Introduction).

For me these words at the heart of the theological vision of Benedict XVI present concisely the Christian vision of hope in the midst of all that would seem to stand in hope's away. In the midst of all that seems hopeless it is our faith in the victory won by Christ through his death and resurrection which grounds us in the truth of the crucified and risen Christ's presence here and now and informs our vision of the new life of the world to come. 'Hope', says Benedict, 'is the virtue without which the disciple cannot move anywhere'. True Christian hope is the foundational theological virtue. It is grounded in faith in our redemption and realized in love but without this hope neither faith nor love can take root.

It is in Benedict's first seminal encyclical *Deus Caritas est,* on Christian love, that we find the basis for his vision of hope. The hope of the Christian is grounded in the relationship between the loving God and us his disciples called to follow his command to love as he did. In the incarnation Christ beckons us out of our unbelief, our confusion, our despair at the world's God-forsakenness as we constantly long to find our hope completed in the gift of the God who has become one of us. It is this longing, the love of desire, the love of eros for God's coming as Beloved, which is the culmination of the drama of human hope. This will be expressed infinitely in the *agape* love with which the Christ we long for gifts our world which in all its raggedness yearns for the embrace of such a God. It is as though God's self and God's beautiful creation is loved into a living communion from which hope springs eternal. God in Christ knows the yearnings of the human heart, the nerve centre of creation, of our world's desire for completion. Our hope is thus assured and joyful.

We live in very troubled times which can easily drive believer and non-believer alike to despair. Many who profess faith in Christ despair at the godlessness of the world, of the abuses of power in institutional Christianity, of structural sin which gives rise to such injustice in society where the poor are punished and the wealthy rewarded in this life. For the Christian believer we can profess our faith but without hope in the goodness of God's redeemed creation we can and do still create disunity both in the Body of Christ and between Christians and secular society. Are we Pope Francis or Pope Benedict Catholics? Are we pro-life or pro-justice? Do we profess that certain hope of which Benedict spoke so powerfully that in the end God will draw all to himself as it is God who creates and sustains us as his beloved creation?

The Canticle of Creation, composed by Saint Francis d'Assisi eight hundred years ago, has inspired generations up to our own to challenge our view of creation, encouraging us to praise God for all that he has created, and to take responsibility to help her to flourish. In *Laudato Si'*, Pope Francis, in our own time of crisis, is encouraging us to renew our hope in a God whose face is to be uncovered in our world. God is in the communion between nature and humanity and we are called to love, respect and protect her just as we, his beautiful creation, are loved by God. Pope Francis' urgent call is rooted as Pope Benedict's call to faith, hope and love, in the saving love of Christ which grounds us in hope that we are redeemed, that as Julian of Norwich famously proclaimed all will be well and all manner of things be well, and that the whole of God's good creation will be consummated at the final judgement. So it is through our living out the command to love as Christ did in his dying for us that true hope inspired by faith takes root in our hearts.

These papal documents, then, present a challenge to our world view, drawing us back to the nature of Christian hope itself. At the start of his pontificate Francis famously said we are not in an era of change but this is a change of era. The call to embrace this new era is urgent. It is often expressed in negative terms lamenting the decline in active Church attendance, in the rise of secularism, in fundamentalist and extremist positions which encourage us to panic. Pope Francis has indeed expressed how urgent the care of creation is to save the planet but this call is rooted in true Christian hope in the goodness of redeemed creation and our responsibility for it. The future is very much in our hands as Christ's Body yet ultimately in the hands of a God who loves us so much he is calling us into closer communion with each other, with our environment, and with himself risen for us.

Fr Dominic Robinson, S.J., Parish Priest of Farm Street Church, Mayfair, London

Bishop John Sherrington

The Flame of Hope

During his baptism, Eddy was attracted and fascinated by the flickering flame of the paschal candle near the font. When Jim took the light from the candle to light the baptismal candle, the priest said, 'Receive the Light of Christ. This light is entrusted to you to be kept burning brightly. This child of yours has been enlightened by Christ. He is to walk always as a child of that light. May he keep the flame of faith alive in his heart. When the Lord comes, may he go out to meet him with all the saints in the heavenly kingdom.' This flame of hope will accompany Eddy through his earthly life towards heaven. In baptism, Eddy becomes a new creation, a member of the Body of Christ, and is called the beloved of the Lord. From faith comes hope: as Cardinal Pierbattista Pizzaballa, the Latin Patriarch of Jerusalem, said, 'Hope is the daughter of faith.' This flame of hope will remind Eddy that Christ has saved his people and walks with them throughout their lives. He will carry the cross with Eddy during days of suffering and illness and will watch over him with love at his death. At the funeral liturgy, the Paschal Candle will burn again near Eddy's coffin as a sign of the promise that 'life is changed not ended' and will be the sign of the hope of eternal life (Cf. Pope Francis, Jubilee Bull of Indiction, *Spes non confundit* 20).

Eddy will face the reality of evil, suffering and death in the future. He is strengthened by the oil of catechumens against this reality. Suffering is a mystery which has preoccupied philosophers and theologians for millennia. Each one of us asks at some time in our lives, 'Why do good people suffer?' Christ gives us an answer which we often struggle to grasp – follow me. God shares fully in our humanity when the Word became flesh and pitched his tent amongst us. He sheds light on the mystery of being human and shows us how to live with suffering. He points us beyond this earthly existence to our life in heaven and reveals his promise of eternal closeness to us (Cf. Gaudium et Spes 22).

When we suffer, we are invited to turn to Christ on the cross with a contemplative gaze of love. On the cross Christ empties himself and descends to the ultimate limits of human weakness, even unto death, but God lifts him up in triumph and exultation (Phil 2:6-11). Although despised and rejected by others, Christ retains his dignity as truly man and truly God.

The triumph of Jesus on the cross makes the flame of hope burn ever more brightly in the darkness of the one who suffers. Saint Paul rejoices in his own sufferings because he knows Christ is victorious: 'More than that, we rejoice in our sufferings, knowing that suffering produces endurance, and endurance produces character, and character produces hope, and hope does not disappoint us, because God's love has been poured into our hearts through the Holy Spirit which has been given to us' (Rom 5:3-5).

Many saints show us that by offering their suffering to the Father, they meet Christ who loves them, is close to them in their trials, and looks upon them with tender love. By his cross Christ has triumphed totally over evil and death; he does not need human suffering to complete his sacrifice. Rather he freely allows the self-offering of others in solidarity with himself to contribute to the healing of the wounds of the world and the Church. The self-offering of suffering is an act of love which is ever fruitful and offers hope to the one who suffers. It transforms them. The workings of God's love are expressed by Saint Paul: 'In my flesh I complete what is lacking in Christ's afflictions for the sake of his body, that is, the Church' (Col 1:24).

This journey calls for the gift of faith and the solidarity of the Christian community around the one who suffers. The invitation to other members of the Church is to be a Good Samaritan and neighbour to the one who suffers. In her liturgical rites, the Church offers the consolation and hope of the Sacrament of the Sick and the nourishment of the *Viaticum*. She also offers prayers for the sick, the dying and those who undergo other forms of suffering. Today we need to rediscover this sense of walking together as pilgrims who hold up our flames of hope and bring light to those who suffer.

The saints reveal that the pathway of human suffering is often a dark night of faith. In the suffering she endured during her short life and with a painful terminal illness, Saint Thérèse of Lisieux could say, 'In the heart of the Church, my Mother, I shall be love… and this my dream will be realized.' She offered her suffering to the Father and through her trust and knowledge of God's love, she became holy and allowed her love to spread out to others and transform the world (Pope Francis, *Dilexit* Nos 198). At the time of our death, Jesus invites us to imitate him and surrender our life into the embrace of the merciful love of the Father, 'Father, into your hands I commit my spirit' (Lk 23:46).

The flame of the Paschal Candle will burn brightly beside the human remains of Christians when they lie in the coffin at their funeral liturgy. Each will wait in the hope of the resurrection to hear the welcoming words of the Father, 'Well done, good and faithful servant; enter the joy of your Master (Mt 25:23). They will have carried the flame of hope faithfully by trusting in the tender mercy of God.

Rt Revd John Sherrington, Auxiliary Bishop of Westminster

Fr Robert Smialek

The Transformative Hope of the Resurrection

A few years ago, I watched a movie on the life Saint Paul. A scene that took place in Rome during Paul's imprisonment, following the struggle of the early Christians who were living through the persecution of Nero was particularly notable. Overall I enjoyed the movie but there was a particular scene that left a deep and troubling impression on me. The scene followed Saint Luke through the streets of Rome; he had just visited Paul in prison, and as he meandered through the streets he stumbles across a fellow Christian tied to a pole drenched in flammable oil. The Christian catches sight of Luke and gestures to him to stay away. As Luke turns back, the camera pans to the wall where you see the silhouette of a Roman solider raising a torch to set the Christian alight. I thought about this scene for months. Whether Luke historically witnessed such an event is irrelevant, for the truth is, many Christians suffered a fate such as this as depicted in the film.

I kept wondering as to what that Christian must have been thinking at the time of his death. Did he feel betrayed by God? Was he disappointed? I even began to question God myself and in my questioning I became angry. I argued to God: this man chose to follow Christ and this is his reward? He believed, he did everything right, he responded in faith as

God wanted him to, so why did his life have to come to such a gruesome end? Why does he who believes suffer and those who don't prosper?

In the hope of an answer, I started to devour the letters of scripture and the life of the saints for insight. I read the writings of Saint Ignatius of Antioch, and the martyrdom of Saints Felicity and Perpetua, I read homilies by Saint John Chrysostom and many, many more. As I delved into the mind of the early Church I began to realize one huge difference between me and those heroic men and women of the early Church. Compared to me, they had real faith! I began to understand that the defining feature that shaped the faith of the early Church wasn't only their belief that Jesus died for our sins, it was the apocalyptic announcement that Jesus rose from the dead! When Our Lord walked out from that tomb, the narrative of human existence and universal creation was rewritten. The resurrection of Jesus Christ ruptured and shattered the narrative of the world. It freed us from a small and narrow minded view of human existence that measured success in terms of money, pleasure and power. It destroyed the idea that death is victorious.

To gaze through the eyes of faith is to see life in a radically new way, it is to view life through the lens of the resurrection. Jesus walking out of that tomb changed everything and those early Christians knew it and we should know this too! Part of our Christian journey then, involves our coming to terms with what the resurrection of Jesus Christ means for our existence and how it shapes the way we live our lives. When Saint Ignatius went to his death in the arena of lions, he viewed his suffering as his final moment to deepen his identification with Christ. He saw his martyrdom as a gift, a new way to know Christ and to participate in his life and he would not be denied it. This deeper union with Christ gained through his martyrdom, wasn't for Ignatius a fleeting moment of final bliss that would end with his death, it was for Ignatius, the final act of union he would perform in this life that would endure into the next. A union that he knew would be made manifest in his resurrected body, endure for all eternity and attain for him the degree by which he would participate in the divine life of God. Such logic makes no sense to the world but to Ignatius and for those Christians who knew the full meaning of the resurrection of Christ, it makes perfect sense. Everything in this life can be used to identify with Christ, everything in this life can be used to deepen our union with Christ. Even suffering and injustice can be used to our advantage because Christ too suffered and experienced injustice. In our darkest moments Christ is there, relatable, knowable, and not even death can separate us from him.

The whole of our Christian life then, ought to be driven by the desire to unite ourselves to Christ through acts of love. For that which we gain in this life, will be brought to glory in our bodies at the resurrection. We don't work for earthly gains anymore, we work for heavenly gains. We live with the hope that springs forth from the knowledge that our bodies will be resurrected and the union we obtain with Christ in this life, will be made manifest in our bodies in the life to come. Every cell of our glorified bodies will be a participation in the divine life of God. When Christ returns to recreate the whole of creation and resurrect our bodies into glory, we will see in each other the degree to which we loved Christ and we will rejoice in each other's glory. We have this faith, we know it to be true, because Christ walked out of that tomb and promised us the same experience thus: "I am the resurrection and the life. Whoever believes in me, though he die, yet shall he live" (Jn 11:25).

Returning then to that Christian I mentioned in my opening paragraph and what was going through his mind at the time of his death, I now think it was nothing short of a miracle that was taking place; I think he was performing one final act of love: he was forgiving them. He forgave them just as Saint Stephen forgave those who were stoning him. He forgave them, so he could identify with Christ one last time, in imitation of Christ's forgiveness from the Cross. In his final moments, in the hope of the resurrection, he united himself to Christ, so as to increase his glory in the resurrection to come. In the eyes of the world his death was a loss; through the eyes of faith, his death was his gain. God, grant me that faith and instil in me the hope of the resurrection.

Fr Robert Smialek, Assistant Pastor, Saint Joseph's, Stevenage and one of the most recently ordained priests in the Diocese of Westminster.

Sandy Walkington

Hope as a Journey

"It is a better thing to travel hopefully than to arrive." So wrote Robert Louis Stevenson.

My first true journey into the unknown was to Cold War Berlin at the age of 18. I had finished school but could not immediately start university; my parents thought I should disappear somewhere but it was up to me to sort something out. I wrote to various businesses with international operations and was offered a job in a factory in West Berlin.

I had never left home before. I had never even been 'abroad' before. I saved enough pocket money for a one-way rail ticket to Berlin and a tiny bit more. I don't recall my parents giving me anything before my brother dropped me at midnight at a gaslit Gloucester station to get the night train to Paddington, and thence to Ostend.

The huge black Ost-West Express - from Ostend to Moscow - took me into the winter. We trundled across a darkening Europe past Koln Cathedral and over the Rhine. It began to snow and we crossed the iron curtain into East Germany in the early hours, the floodlights lighting the flakes, and frontier guards in greatcoats, rifles slung across their shoulders, stamping the snow off their boots as they came into the compartment to inspect our travel documents. More frontier stuff, more high barbed wire fences, more lights as we entered the snowy enclave of West Berlin.

Zoo Station, dark and cavernous. I get off the train. A man with a brochure with the company name. "Herr Walkington?" "Ja", my schoolboy German kicking in. He led me down to a car and we drove off through snowy streets, different architecture, yellow buses, I plucked up courage, "Mein Herr, wo fahren wir hin? Sir, where are we going?" Without looking at me, his teeth clenched as he carefully avoided skidding, he said "Me spik no English."

The next few days were a whirlwind of getting work permits and finding somewhere for me to live, a studio flat in the American sector of Berlin. It was the red light district, a strip club in the basement; I was armoured by innocence - there wasn't a red light district in the Gloucestershire town where I grew up.

The factory was in the British sector. The cheapest way of getting there was by the S-Bahn suburban rail service operated by East Berlin who invested as little as possible in the West Berlin service, and whose pre-war tracks ignored the political geography of the streets above. So my ancient train lurched underground almost immediately after I caught it, under the Wall into the Russian sector, now East Berlin. Empty stations with one or two neon lights and armed soldiers to ensure no-one escaped. The occasional spark from the third rail in the tunnels revealing more soldiers. Changing trains in the middle of East Berlin at Friedrichstrasse station. Coming up to the surface to a station with a wall running down the middle. On one side trains going to Warsaw and Moscow, on our side trains to West Berlin and a soldier with a gun silhouetted in the roof making sure no-one followed their hopes and escaped. And then we proceeded between barbed wire fences and watch towers to the Berlin Wall proper, the sand covered killing strip, the line of concrete, and then the still empty Reichstag and the west. My first daily commute.

The factory made and anodized aluminium door and window frames. I was the only West European in a gang of Turks loading lorries. Our boss was a self-confessed Nazi who told me she had sworn to Hitler on his final birthday that she would fight to the death to save the Fatherland. I asked what had happened. "It wasn't fair - they crept up behind me when I wasn't looking." She hated the British - we had bombed her city to bits and then in the immediate aftermath of the war a soldier in a Schottenrock - a kilt - had stood guard over her while she had to shovel coal after walking miles across a shattered city in the snow.

My Turkish co-workers were fascinated by me. "England rich country, why you work here?" Their own journey to Germany had been one of hope for a better life. In their own way they were very kind, it gave me a lasting respect and affection for people of the Muslim faith.

We really were the lowest of the low, I was treated as an honorary Turk - the last to get safety equipment and the accident rate was appalling, I had my hand crushed by a drunken crane operator (there were beer machines in the canteen). One day an international conference delegation came to visit the factory. We were all told to climb into a canvas-sided lorry trailer out in the yard and stay out of sight until they left.

May Day was a holiday. As a British passport holder I was allowed into the East (West Berliners were not with families cruelly divided). I crossed over and went to stand on Unter den Linden to watch the parade, much of which had passed by the time I got there and it was just great phalanxes of people tiredly chanting 'DDR hoch hoch hoch! All power to East Germany" as they shuffled by.

Suddenly a Vopo, a "people's policeman", shoved me in the back and said 'Marschieren! March'. I found myself behind a red banner "Lokomotiv Leipzig No. 3", my co-marchers hopelessly repeating 'DDR hoch hoch hoch!' while I muttered 'God save the Queen, God save the Queen'. We proceeded down Unter den Linden, past the People's Palace on our right where the royal palace used to be, the still semi-ruined cathedral on the left, and then swung right into the brand new Alexanderplatz where the Praesidium was taking the salute.

So assuming they had not already disappeared for a slap-up meal, Ernst Honecker the new leader and Walter Ulbricht the still living founder of East Germany were there to receive the salute from a sullen bunch of Leipzigers and an 18-year-old from Gloucestershire. My wanderings in East Germany and other travels in former East European nations showed me the corrosiveness of national hopelessness.

Much later at a wildly expensive leadership course at Oxford University where I sat between an Anglican bishop and an army brigadier, a US staff colonel drummed into us that 'Hope is not a Strategy'. But by gosh it helps.

The complete Stevenson quote is 'It is a better thing to travel hopefully than to arrive, and the true success is to labour." My strange work experience in Berlin was more joy than pain, 'Laborare est orare' (to work is to pray). I still work part-time in my 70s. 'Dum spiro spero' (while I breathe I hope).

Sandy Walkington, Hertfordshire politician and speaker.

Francesca Weal

Building Hope

Hope is manifest in a building project. It is an essential characteristic without which the project cannot be completed. It is hope in the future that drives a project's inception: the future of a home, a business, a church, a community, a city or a nation. There is hope in shaping the direction of the building.

The first task is to think into the future and see what shape the project will take. What are we doing this for? Where are we planning to site it? What is the hoped-for pattern of occupation or commercial process? What finance do we think we can raise? How do we want the building to show our purpose to the world at large?

Building a new church or otherwise engaging in a substantial reordering and extension is a great expression of hope. It is a veritable 'leap of faith' both in the secular and religious meaning. Is faith then hope? There is hope that the people will come and continue to come in the future; that the church will be a focus for the church community and welcoming to all: believers and non-believers alike. There is hope that funds will be forthcoming. There is hope that the project will clear considerable statutory and ecclesiastical requirements. There is hope that it will meet expectations.

The next task is to assemble the team to enable the project. All members of the team have to share the hope but also be realistic about achievable aims. It is at this point I get involved in building projects and as an architect I feel the enormity of the hope. The task is to coalesce all the elements of the brief into a vision, from the initial hand sketches through to a scheme ready for initial consultation. The hope is that it will be visionary, have liturgical meaning, affordable and acceptable to the parish and the relevant authorities. This is particularly complex when works are proposed for a listed building.

Churches need to get the project to a stage at which fundraising can commence in earnest. For them, the commitment of fees to the early stages of the project demonstrates their hope in its success. Some take this even further. I was on an EASA[1] tour which visited a west country church which had just completed a major reordering and the vicar described how they were still fundraising as the project was under construction. The results were very good – a testament to their hope and tenacity.

The planning process can be a trial of patience and hope. The system can be somewhat random in its outcome. I recall one of our projects was initially refused by a very small committee, despite a recommendation for approval, mainly due to wanting an increase in parking even though we'd complied with local policies: the concern being the potential size of Catholic families. I recall hearing 'you know what they are like'. The parish priest lost half his garden to cars, then it cleared the next committee. Ironically however, church attendance greatly increased beyond planned expectations after the new church was built and the cark park is often stuffed.

With heritage buildings, there are also additional tensions and conflicts to resolve arising from comments from secular consultees and diocesan consultees.

The next stage is the technical design. The hope is to design where possible to the budget but allowing for the unexpected. For one project we commissioned a ground penetrating radar survey to locate unmarked interments at the site of proposed church extension. We are now in the technical design phase: setting out piles and foundations. We hope that all burials have been found – but there is always the risk of 'disarticulated remains' being found nonetheless. Working with existing buildings is particularly risky. But pre-construction investigations and surveys help reduce the risk.

The last stage is the physical realization of hope. The hope is for a smooth tender process; a project 'coming in' on or near to a budget; hope for a construction phase that runs smoothly. It is worth understanding that reputable building contractors also invest 'hope' in a project. They hope that their bid was not so low that they lose money and risk becoming insolvent. They also look forward to building something of value of which they can feel proud: this is true from director level down to the site workforce.

For me, the construction process is the action of bringing order out of chaos, with the hope that the expectations of the parish are realized. It is the hope and trust in one's own ability to solve inevitable site problems. I had a particularly difficult project which included complex extensions and refurbishment of a large village hall and meeting rooms. It was tendered and accepted just before Putin invaded Ukraine; that and changes in trading with the EU and COVID, all played havoc with supply lines. But the parish councillor driving the project had had the vision and hope to push it through and managed to secure a very good interest deal just before interest rates soared. So we staggered through it all; I just had to hope we could deal with the roller-coaster of product availability and endless 'value-engineering'. We did.

The final outcome is occupation. I cannot get over the feeling of awe as I stand inside something that was a few rough lines on a sketching pad a few years before. These days 3D visualizations take away some of the mental 'leap of faith' in the realization of a project, but they never get the materiality of a scheme: the micro-choices of type of mortar (mostly lime now for me), sand, wood species, paint finishes; how the changing light during the day comes through the carefully placed windows and rooflights.

It is such a wonderful feeling to see how the whole team, client, consultants and contractors, has given a shape to the hope. I recall saying to a contractor that he needed to realize that the church he was building was to be built to last. I said that funds for this were being raised by school children, some of whom may still be going to that church for the rest of their lives.

That is hope indeed.

Francesca Weal
Church & Conservation Architect

Fr Nigel Woollen

All or Nothing

Rising from the Ashes

Paris, January 2019: I find myself outside Notre-Dame Cathedral, which I'd previously visited several times. There's a long queue of tourists waiting to enter; I say to myself, I'll go in next time.

There was no next time. Three months later, on 15 April, fire severely damaged the cathedral, forcing its closure for five years. No one was killed - a firefighter and two police officers were injured - but the symbolic status of Notre-Dame for the city of Paris, for the French nation (believers and non-believers alike) and countless others beyond its borders, was such that it felt like a tragedy, an utter disaster.

I think of the London parish church I currently serve, destroyed by bombing in 1940 (with extensive loss of life) then rebuilt and reopened to much fanfare in 1959. My Irish friends would recall another fire which destroyed a cathedral - in Longford - on Christmas Day 2009, restored in 2014. The happy ending to the Notre-Dame saga was its joyful reopening on 8 December 2024, to immense international interest. The date is symbolic: the Feast of the Immaculate Conception is one held in great esteem by French Catholics, since Our Lady introduced herself by this title to Saint Bernadette in Lourdes, in 1858. Sadness gives way to joy, despair to hope, death to new life. *Disaster leading to triumph: isn't this the Christian message in a nutshell?*

I often reflect on grief, not in a morbid way, but as a human reality none of us can escape. Like many priests, I have had the honour and challenge of celebrating my parents' funerals; quite a few of my closest friends have recently lost a parent, and I said farewell this year to Craig, a college acquaintance for nearly 40 years, who passed away after a courageous battle with Motor Neurone Disease. I was touched when his wife asked me to conduct his funeral service; he wasn't a Catholic but a sincere and compassionate Christian, who with great reverence accepted the Sacrament of the Sick I offered him not long before he died. However, a particular kind of grief I will never know is that of a parent who has lost a child; it's hard to imagine the wound this must cause in the soul of a mother or father thus affected. One would certainly acknowledge their right to cry to the Lord: *Why did you allow this to happen?*

The Young Ones

The Bible gives many glimpses of hope for those who ask, *why so much suffering?* A wonderful promise is found in the prophet Jeremiah: "I know the plans I have for you, says the Lord, plans for welfare and not for evil, to give you a future and a hope" (Jer 29:11). Also, the lives of the saints can help those in pain and sorrow; their stories inspire us to journey towards healing and grow in an awareness of the Lord's *plans for our welfare.* The story of Saint Josephine Bakhita - kidnapped in Sudan as a young girl and sold as a slave, before ending up in Italy and becoming a Catholic nun - reminds us that nothing is impossible to God. We can barely grasp the grief of her loved ones who never saw her again, yet her own firm and serene conviction that the events permitted by God enabled her to discover the Catholic faith inspires us to trust that he can bring good out of the direst situations.

The abundance of *young* saints or saints-in-waiting the Church invites us to imitate and call upon - of whom two, Pier-Giorgio Frassati and London-born Carlo Acutis, will be canonized in 2025 - should make us aware that their passing, while certainly seen as a tragedy by their parents and family members, is somehow part of God's ineffable designs, and an inspiration to us to seek fresh insight with regard to all that appears negative or senseless. Pier-Giorgio died at 24, Carlo at 15; we can also cite Blessed Chiara Badano who passed away at 18 (these three all died of illness) and Sister Clare Crockett (the original 'Derry Girl') killed in an earthquake in Ecuador aged 33; her cause for beatification was recently opened. Unimaginable grief for their loved ones, yet grace and blessing for countless believers inspired by their stories. Sister Clare's motto *All or Nothing* recalls the words of Saint John of the Cross:

> *To reach satisfaction in all, desire satisfaction in nothing.*
> *To come to possess all, desire the possession of nothing.*
> *To arrive at being all, desire to be nothing.*
> *To come to the knowledge of all, desire the knowledge of nothing.*
>
> ('Ascent of Mount Carmel', book 1, chapter 13, n 11)

This seems completely countercultural and impossible to achieve for us mere mortals, but simply echoes and expands upon the words of Jesus: "None of you can be my disciple unless he gives up all his possessions" (Lk 14:33). Not the favourite biblical quote for most of us, yet once again the saints show us what really matters: striving to let go of our hunger for possessions, pleasures and power, we can find something much greater, a pathway to achieve freedom and true happiness. "If you find your delight in the Lord, he will grant your heart's desire" (Ps 36:4).

Finding Purpose

Ultimately, the answer to every profound question on the meaning of life - finding purpose in what seems to be purposelessness, claiming hope in situations of apparent hopelessness - is the Cross of Christ. There, we find the greatest injustice ever committed, the darkest day in human history - putting to death in painful fashion the very Son of God and Saviour of the world, who came that we may have life, and have it to the full (cf. Jn 10:10) - yet, a day which is called in the old English tradition, Good Friday (an adjective not found in other languages), since God is an expert at bringing good out of evil.

The saints tell us: Yes, there is hope, there is meaning! Beyond the vale of tears, a new light will shine. "You have kept an account of my tears, are they not written in your book?" (Ps 55:8) Mary, who stood sorrowfully by the Cross (cf. Jn 19:25-27) yet waited in hope for her Son's resurrection, continues to watch over her suffering children anticipating the day of glory for each one, when by his great mercy we shall at last receive "all that God has prepared for those who love him" (1 Cor 2:9).

May the pain and suffering of all people of good will not be in vain; may the efforts of believers to reflect the loving-kindness of our Saviour for others bring forth abundant fruit; may we never doubt that God is with us. "May your love be upon us, O Lord, as we place all our hope in you" (Ps 32:8).

Fr Nigel Woollen Author and Parish Priest of Our Lady of Victories Church, Kensington High Street.

Richard Jacques

Can We See Hope?

Artists and philosophers have long struggled with questions of what art is for and how it shapes our experience as viewers. When it comes to sacred art the answers to these questions may seem more obvious, for here an artwork is usually required to illuminate some aspect of our faith and spark in us a devotional and prayerful response. Many will recognize the feelings of sorrow, grief and possibly even guilt when we look upon an image of Jesus suffering on the cross. Likewise, when confronted with paintings of Christian martyrs we may experience in our own bodies a sense of their pain and anguish, in a similar manner to the empathy we feel for the pain of others in our daily lives as we visit family who are sick or watch the never-ending human tragedies that dominate the nightly television news. Yet, for all that art can hold a mirror to the more painful aspects of our lives, the more challenging emotions to depict in paint or stone are surely the brighter but less tangible feelings of joy, love and most especially hope.

As an art historian my working days are spent trying to understand how works of art were created and how they speak to those, both past and present, who encounter them. However, even with a trained eye I cannot hide the difficulty in seeing hope, an emotion that is both intensely internal and individual. Our personal hopes and dreams are as unique as the pattern of our eyes or the lines on the palms of our hands. Hope also inevitably points toward a future state of being that is distinctly better than our current life. To portray this ineffable emotion, artists must therefore deploy the cleverest of techniques and pictorial strategies to reveal something so hidden in the human heart, producing artworks that are capable of engaging the viewer in both our present reality and our desire for what is yet to come. Here the makers of Christian art may have an advantage over their purely secular counterparts, for the Church has long held that the highest purpose of religious art is to use the artist's God given talents to direct the beholder towards events and beliefs whose meanings lie quite rightly beyond our material world. As the writer of Ecclesiastes so eloquently explains, 'He has made everything beautiful in its time. Also, he has put eternity into man's heart, yet so that he cannot find out what God has done from the beginning to the end.' (Eccl 3:11). Whether through painting, sculpture, music, or literature, sacred art should therefore transcend barriers and open windows to a world where hope is not only visible but tangible.

One painting that for me encapsulates this potential of quite literally seeing hope is this image of Mary worshiping the Christ Child by the Italian seventeenth century artist Giovanni Battista Salvi, better known as Sassoferrato (1609-1665). Here the artist depicts the Virgin Mary in quiet adoration of the Christ Child, who is resting on a white cloth before her. The Virgin's hands are clasped in prayer, her head inclined with a gentle, contemplative expression. Sassoferrato emphasizes Mary's purity and devotion through the soft, unblemished features of her face set against the vivid ultramarine of her cloak. The Christ Child is painted with a tender realism, his posture exuding innocence and vulnerability, while the interplay of light and shadow highlights the sacred intimacy between mother and child. Sassoferrato's deliberate use of smooth textures and vibrant colours creates a luminous, almost otherworldly quality. A restrained approach, focusing on stillness and devotion that invites the viewer to meditate on the divine mystery of the Nativity

One of art's most profound abilities is to remind us of the extraordinary beauty in the ordinary, and nothing can be more familiar than the relationship between a mother and her child. In Sassoferrato's painting we see clearly that most intimate bond of a mother's unconditional love and a child's total trust and dependence. A tender moment in which Mary is the Christ Child's whole world. An image that fosters hope through its connection to our shared humanity. An encounter through the medium of paint that echoes our own struggles or joys, and a reminder of that moment when looking into our own mother's eye we realized that we are not alone. A sense of belonging that is profoundly hopeful.

One detail of Sassoferrato's painting that might easily be missed is the neatly rolled up piece of cloth lying by the Child's feet. At first glance this may appear as a swaddling cloth, that will soon be used to clothe the naked infant's body. Yet as we dwell on this perfectly depicted object our thoughts may well be cast forward to the clothes that Mary will use some years in the future to wrap her dead son as he is taken down from the cross. The cloth witnessed by Simon Peter as he entered the empty tomb 'that had been on Jesus' head, not lying with the linen wrappings but rolled up in a place by itself' (Jn 20:7). A simple roll of linen transformed into the greatest symbol of our Christian hope.

Ultimately, the hope found in art lies in its affirmation of life's depth and potential. It speaks to our resilience, creativity, and capacity for joy even in the darkest times. By engaging with art, we find reminders of both God's grace in our own lives and glimpses of a world worth striving for—a world, both present and future where hope persists, radiant and unyielding.

Richard Jacques, Art Historian

Sassoferrato, Mary worshipping the Christ Child, c.1640-60, Städel Museum, Frankfurt am Main

Archbishop Joseph Marino

A Call to Be Pilgrims of Hope

Introduction

On 13 May 2024, which was Ascension Thursday, Pope Francis announced that the Church would celebrate a Jubilee Year in 2025. In the Bull in which he proclaimed the Holy Year, entitled, *Spes non Confundit* (SC), that is, "Hope does not disappoint" (Rom 5:5), he wrote: "In the spirit of hope, the Apostle Paul addressed these words of encouragement to the Christian community of Rome. Hope is also the central message of the coming Jubilee that, in accordance with an ancient tradition, the Pope proclaims every twenty-five years" (SC n 1).

With these words, the Holy Father confirms a tradition in the Church, dating back to 1300, to celebrate a Jubilee Year, which in these latest times has been every 25 years, the last Ordinary Jubilee Year being the year, 2000. Pope Francis declared that the point of reflection and action for this special time of grace, the Jubilee Year 2025, would be hope.

In the opening paragraph of this document, Pope Francis reminds us that the Holy Year, as always, is lived within the dynamic of a pilgrimage, a movement, a journey leading to transformation and renewal. In that regard, he stated: "My thoughts turn to all those *pilgrims of hope* who will travel to Rome in order to experience the Holy Year and to all those others who, though unable to visit the City of the Apostles

Peter and Paul, will celebrate it in their local Churches" (SC n 1).

The Jubilee of 2025: Awaking hope arising from faith

Pope Francis confirmed the Jubilee Year of 2025 within the context of the celebration of Vespers or Evening Prayer of the Ascension, during which he preached a homily reflecting on the spiritual significance of this year of grace. Therefore, we have two sources for our understanding of this Jubilee: the Bull (SC), mentioned above and the *homily* given at Vespers (AT).

In both instances, the Holy Father offers the deep significance of hope, first within the context of the actual state of the world.

He recalls that we live in "a culture marked by much despair" … "often caught up only in the present and incapable of looking to the future "… (We live) "in an age caught up in an individualism that is frequently content merely to scrape along from day to day. Peoples and nations look to the future with anxiety and fear," because "injustice and arrogance persist, the poor are discarded, wars sow seeds of death, the least of our brothers and sisters remain at the bottom of the pile, and the dream of a fraternal world seems an illusion." Young people live in a state of confusion and uncertainty longing for a life of happiness and fulfilment. The elderly, the sick and the suffering live with a sense of being abandoned "by a culture obsessed with efficiency and excess." Even creation, the world itself, "gravely damaged and disfigured by human selfishness" survives with a sense of need and yearning (AT).

In short, Pope Francis sees the present state of the world - and even the Church - as a time of great "uncertainty about the future" which "gives rise to conflicting feelings, ranging from confident trust to apprehensiveness, from serenity to anxiety, from firm conviction to hesitation and doubt." In that context, therefore, he writes: "Often we come across people who are discouraged, pessimistic and cynical about the future, as if nothing could possibly bring them happiness" (SC, n 1).

Consequently, our lives so often are "weary and wounded, our hearts thirsting for truth, goodness and beauty, and our dreams that no darkness can dispel" (AT).

In this context, we can say "everything, within and outside of us, cries out for hope" .. What we – all of us – need, then, is hope", not mere human hope, which is mere "human" optimism or the ephemeral expectation of some earthly benefit" (AT).

Rather, our yearnings are based on Christian hope, which "sustains the journey of our lives, even when the road ahead seems winding and exhausting. It opens our eyes to future possibilities whenever resignation or pessimism attempt to imprison us. It makes us see the promise of good at times when evil seems to prevail. Christian hope fills us with serenity when our hearts are burdened by sin and failure. It makes us dream of a new humanity and gives us courage in our efforts to build a fraternal and peaceful world, even when it seems barely worth the effort" (AT).

Christian hope, then is not a philosophical or abstract reflection. Rather it is something real that has already been accomplished through the mission of Christ and given to us at Baptism (AT).

Christian hope arises from our response to the redemptive mission of Christ himself, who died and rose from the dead. In other words, there is a connection between faith and hope, so much so, that often in the Sacred Scriptures faith and hope are interchangeable. Faith gives us hope; our hope comes from faith. Pope Benedict XVI, in his Encyclical on hope, *Spe salvi* (SS) (in hope we are saved), teaches how Saint Paul explains this beautifully in his Letter to the Ephesians. "Paul reminded the Ephesians that before their encounter with Christ they were "without hope and without God in the world" (*Eph* 2:12). Of course, he knew that they had had gods, he knew that they had had a religion, but their gods had proved questionable, and no hope emerged from their mythical gods. Their gods notwithstanding, they were "without God" and consequently found themselves in a dark world, facing a dark future" (SS n 2).

But for Christians, when we encounter Christ and embrace him in faith, we know that there is a future, that is, we have hope that opens the door to a future even if we do not know all its details. We know that life does not lead to emptiness or oblivion.

The future is a positive reality, not an illusion or a fantasy. This hope is based on our relationship with Christ. Consequently, it must be noted that at the very beginning of the Bull on the Jubilee Year, Pope Francis hopes that: "For everyone, may the Jubilee be a moment of genuine, personal encounter with the Lord Jesus, the "door" (cf. Jn 10:7.9) of our salvation, whom the Church is charged to proclaim always, everywhere and to all as "our hope" (1 *Tim* 1:1)" (SC, n 1).

It is a call which the Holy Father made at the very beginning of his Pontificate in the document, Joy of the Gospel (EG), where, he wrote: "I invite all Christians, everywhere, at this very moment, to a renewed personal encounter with Jesus Christ, or at least an openness to letting him encounter them; I ask all of you to do this unfailingly each day. No one should think that this invitation is not meant for him or her, 'since no one is excluded from the joy brought by the Lord' (Paul VI, Apostolic Exhortation, *Gaudete in Domino*). The Lord does not disappoint those who take this risk" (EG n 3). Indeed, those who accept his offer of salvation are set free from sin, sorrow, inner emptiness and loneliness (EG n 1). In other words, our relationship with Christ, that is faith, gives us hope, gives us a future, gives us a reason for living.

Our faith is not merely a revelation of things and mysteries that can be known—it makes things happen and is life-changing. The dark door of time, of the future, has been thrown open. The one who has faith and hope lives differently; the one who hopes has been granted the gift of a new life (SS n 2).

The Jubilee: Activities to awaken hope

The Jubilee Year offers us this opportunity to renew, to reboot and, if need be, to start over our relationship with Christ through the various spiritual exercises offered to us during this time of grace. Above all it is marked by the '*pilgrimage*' concept, a journey, leading to conversion. Pope Francis wrote: "A *pilgrimage* is of course a fundamental element of every Jubilee event. Setting out on a journey is traditionally associated with our human quest for meaning in life. A pilgrimage on foot is a great aid for rediscovering the value of silence, effort and simplicity of life. In the coming year, pilgrims of hope will surely travel the ancient and more modern routes in order to experience the Jubilee to the full. In Rome itself, along with the usual visits to the catacombs and the Seven Churches, other itineraries of faith will be proposed. Journeying from one country to another as if borders no longer mattered, and passing from one city to another in contemplating the beauty of creation and masterpieces of art, we learn to treasure the richness of different experiences and cultures, and are inspired to lift up that beauty, in prayer, to God, in thanksgiving for his wondrous works. The Jubilee Churches along the pilgrimage routes particularly in the city of Rome can serve as oases of spirituality and places of rest on the pilgrimage of faith, where we can drink from the wellsprings of hope, above all by approaching the sacrament of Reconciliation, the essential starting point of any true journey of conversion" (SC n 5).

With regard to the Jubilee Year of 2025, the Holy Father refers to the very special symbol of every Jubilee, namely the *Holy Doors* of the major Basilicas in Rome. He wrote: "Now the time has come for a new Jubilee, when once more the Holy Door will be flung open to invite everyone to an intense experience of the love of God that awakens in hearts the sure hope of salvation in Christ. The Holy Year will also guide our steps towards yet another fundamental celebration for all Christians: 2033 will mark the 2000th anniversary of the redemption won for us by the passion, death and resurrection of the Lord Jesus. We are about to make a pilgrimage marked by great events, in which the grace of God precedes and accompanies his people as they press forward firm in faith, active in charity and steadfast in hope (cf. 1 *Thess* 1:13)" (SC n 6). As he stated at the very beginning of the Bull, he referred to the passage from John's Gospel which declares Jesus as the door to salvation (Jn 10:7).

Another important spiritual element of the Jubilee Year is the granting of the indulgence. Pope Francis offered a lovely reflection on indulgences for the Extraordinary Jubilee of Mercy in 2015. On that occasion he stated that "a jubilee entails indulgences" (*Misericordiae Vultus,* MV n

22), and he attached an important significance to this practice. The Pope taught that when we are forgiven, "the conflicting consequences of our sins remain" and "sin leaves a negative effect on the way we think and act" (MV n 22). Yet, the mercy of God who "never tires of forgiving in ways that are continually new and surprising", is stronger than the lingering effects of sin. It happens through "the indulgence on the part of the Father who, through the Bride of Christ, his Church, reaches the pardoned sinner and frees him from every residue left by the consequences of sin, enabling him to act with charity, to grow in love rather than to fall back into sin" (MV n 22).

The Holy Father went on to explain that "to live the indulgence of the Holy Year means to approach the Father's mercy with the certainty that his forgiveness extends to the entire life of the believer. To gain an indulgence is to experience the holiness of the Church, who bestows upon all the fruits of Christ's redemption, so that God's love and forgiveness may extend everywhere. Let us live the Jubilee intensely, begging the Father to forgive our sins and to bathe us in his merciful "indulgence"" (MV n 22).

The Jubilee: Signs of Hope

With this new impulse of hope emanating from a renewed relation with Christ arising from the spiritual practices of the Jubilee Year, with the clarity of our vision of reality and life, we can, not only see signs of hope, but we become *singers* and *promoters* of hope. Our spiritual renewal leads us to become instruments of hope in our daily lives.

Pope Francis tells us that "the first sign of hope should be the desire for peace in our world, which once more finds itself immersed in the tragedy of war" (SC n 8).

Another sign of hope moves us to embrace life and encourage the transmission of life. Oftentimes, there is a hesitation in bringing new life into the world because of lack of job security, economic welfare to support a family, causing an alarming decline in population in many countries. Therefore, the Holy Father calls upon the Christian community to be at the forefront in pointing out the need for a *social covenant to support and foster hope,* one that is inclusive and not ideological, working for a future filled with the laughter of babies and children, in order to fill the empty cradles in so many parts of our world (SC n 9).

Moreover, writes the Holy Father, we are called to be tangible signs of hope for those of our brothers and sisters who experience hardships of any kind. He said: "I think of prisoners who, deprived of their freedom, daily feel the harshness of detention and its restrictions, lack of affection and, in more than a few cases, lack of respect for their person." He recalls the Jubilee of the Mosaic Law, written in the Scriptures whose words remain timely yesterday, today and tomorrow (see above), called for the liberation of all every 50 years. Jesus himself took the words of the Prophet Isaiah upon himself when at the beginning of his ministry he said: "The Lord has sent me to bring good news to the oppressed, to bind up the broken-hearted, to proclaim liberty to the captives and release to the prisoners, to proclaim the year of the Lord's favour" (SC n 10).

Pope Francis further pointedly wrote: "In every part of the world, believers, and their Pastors in particular, should be one in demanding dignified conditions for those in prison, respect for their human rights and above all the abolition of the death penalty, a provision at odds with Christian faith and one that eliminates all hope of forgiveness and rehabilitation. In order to offer prisoners a concrete sign of closeness, I would myself like to open a Holy Door in a prison, as a sign inviting prisoners to look to the future with hope and a renewed sense of confidence" (SC n 10).

The Holy Father calls us to give signs of hope to those who are sick, especially those with severe illnesses (SC n 11). Signs of hope are to be given to the young who too often "see their dreams and aspirations frustrated." We must never forget that the young are the future of society and of the Church (SC n 12). Hope is to be extended to the elderly who can be living in situations of loneliness and fear (SC n 14).

In a particular appeal, His Holiness calls upon Christians to offer signs of hope to migrants who leave their homelands behind in search of a better life for themselves and for their families. Their expectations must not be frustrated by prejudice and rejection. A spirit of welcome, which embraces everyone with respect for his or her dignity, should be accompanied by a sense of responsibility, lest anyone be denied the right to a dignified existence (SC n 13).

In a heartfelt appeal, Pope Francis wrote: "I ask with all my heart that hope be granted to the billions of the poor, who often lack the essentials of life. Before the constant tide of new forms of impoverishment, we can easily grow inured and resigned. Yet we must not close our eyes to the dramatic situations that we now encounter all around us, maybe those who live next to us" (SC n 15).

He goes on to make other appeals, in this case to the rich nations asking them to recall that the benefits of the goods of the earth are not destined for a few but for all. In the same context, he asked the affluent nations to acknowledge the gravity of so many of their past decisions and determine to *forgive the debts* of countries that will never be able to repay them. More than a question of generosity, this is a matter of justice (SC n 16).

Jubilee Year: Anchored in hope

Finally, when all is said and done, the ultimate profession of hope is found in our profession of faith, in our Creed, which we profess each Sunday and on every Solemnity: "I believe in *life everlasting*" ... Christian hope finds in these words an essential foundation. For hope is "that theological virtue by which we desire… eternal life as our happiness" (*Catechism of the Catholic Church* n 1817) (SC n 19).

The Pope goes on to say, and how profound as we count time, years and weeks and days, like every twenty-five years… "by virtue of the hope in which we were saved, we can view the passage of time with the certainty that the history of humanity and our own individual history are not doomed to a dead end or a dark abyss, but directed to an encounter with the Lord of glory" at our individual judgement at his second coming (SC n 10).

With regard to judgement, our own and that at the end of time, the Holy Father brings us to the Sistine Chapel and to the great work of Michelangelo which has the aim of inspiring a sense of awe in the viewer. The Pope writes that "we should indeed prepare ourselves consciously and soberly for the moment when our lives will be judged, but we must always do this from the standpoint of hope, the theological virtue that sustains our lives and shields them from groundless fear. The judgement of God, who is love (cf. 1 *Jn* 4:8.16), will surely be based on love, and in particular on all that we have done or failed to do with regard to those in need, in whose midst Christ, the Judge himself, is present (cf. *Mt* 25:31-46). Clearly, then, we are speaking of a judgement unlike any handed down by human, earthly tribunals; it should be understood as a rapport of truth with the God who is love and with oneself, within the unfathomable mystery of divine mercy" (SC n 22). Benedict XVI too affirmed: "At the moment of judgement we experience and we absorb the overwhelming power of his love over all the evil in the world and in ourselves. The pain of love becomes our salvation and our joy" (SS n 47)

Conclusion

The Jubilee Year is a great gift to the Church and even to the world. It invites us to come to terms with time, the rhythm of time, the passing of our lives always with the goal of starting anew, setting the accounts straight, giving ourselves through the ministry of the Church new chances and when necessary, starting over.

This reality is the focus of the Jubilee of 2025, a time of hope, based not on some lofty human and philosophical reflection, but based on a real and personal encounter with the person of Jesus in whom alone can we have a future full of hope, trust and confidence. Only in Jesus and the vision of life that he gave can our true aspirations be fulfilled. Only in him can the authentic desires of life be reached. Only with our pilgrimage with him on earth can we become singers and instruments of hope which the world so dearly needs.

Pope Francis wrote: "In our journey towards the Jubilee, let us return to Scripture and realize that it speaks to us in these words: 'May we who have taken refuge in him be strongly encouraged to seize the hope set before us. We have this hope, a sure and steadfast anchor of the soul, a hope that enters the inner shrine behind the curtain, where Jesus, a forerunner on our behalf, has entered' (Heb 6:18-20). "Those words are a forceful encouragement for us never to lose the hope we have been given, to hold fast to that hope and to find in God our refuge and our strength" (SC n 25).

His Excellency Most Reverend Joseph Marino, President Emeritus of the Pontifical Ecclesiastical Academy.